GoodNews
OF THE
Kingdom
Coming

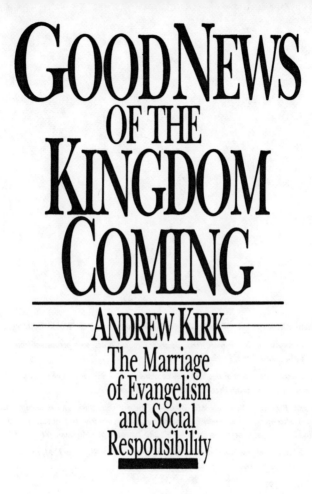

Andrew Kirk

The Marriage
of Evangelism
and Social
Responsibility

InterVarsity Press
DOWNERS GROVE, ILLINOIS 60515

InterVarsity Press is the book-publishing division of Inter-Varsity Christian Fellowship, a student movement active on campus at hundreds of universities, colleges and schools of nursing. For information about local and regional activities, write IVCF, 233 Langdon St., Madison, WI 53703.

Distributed in Canada through InterVarsity Press, 860 Denison St., Unit 3, Markham, Ontario L3R 4H1, Canada.

ISBN 0-87784-938-2

Printed in the United States of America

Library of Congress Cataloging in Publication Data

Kirk, J. Andrew.
    Good news of the kingdom coming.

    Previously published as: A new world coming.
    Bibliography: p.
    Includes index.
    1. Christianity—20th century—Addresses, essays,
lectures. I. Title.
BR123.K539   1985   270.8'2   84-19293
ISBN 0-87784-938-2

17	16	15	14	13	12	11	10	9	8	7	6	5	4	3	2	1
98	97	96	95	94	93	92	91	90	89	88	87	86	85			

To Gillian, companion for life
and telling critic
of all mere theorising

Abbreviations

ARCIC	Anglican–Roman Catholic International Commission
CIIR	Catholic Institute for International Relations
ET	*Expository Times*
GNP	Gross National Product
IBMR	*International Bulletin of Missionary Research*
IMF	International Monetary Fund
IRM	*International Review of Mission*
NEB	New English Bible
RSV	Revised Standard Version
TEV	Today's English Version
UNCTAD	United Nations Commission on Trade and Development
WEF	World Evangelical Fellowship

Preface

I would like to express my thanks to John Hunt of Marshalls for inviting me to expand an article I wrote in 1980 into a full-length book. Originally called 'The Kingdom, the Church and a Distressed World', the article was commissioned by the editor of the *Churchman* as a preparatory reflection on two important mission conferences that took place that year: one in Melbourne and the other in Pattaya, Thailand.

Some of the material I have used in this book has already been presented orally to students of the new London Institute for Contemporary Christianity. It has been modified in the light of their reaction. I would like to thank them collectively for their keen attention and the sharp questions that they posed to some of the themes I developed. Other material has been used in addresses and seminars I have been engaged in, both in Britain and overseas, in connection with my work with the Church Missionary Society. I have learnt much through discussing ideas with people more informed than I; they are too numerous to name individually.

I would like to say, however, how grateful I am to Professor Howard Marshall of Aberdeen University for reading and commenting on Chapter 4 and to Mr Roy McCloughry, Director of the Shaftesbury Project, for doing the same for Chapters 5–7. Howard is a biblical scholar of international repute; Roy is a professional economist. It has been extremely helpful to have them as long-stops to pick up and return the worst of my errors and reckless ideas. Needless to say, they are entirely free of any blame for what appears here.

All quotations from the Bible are from TEV, unless otherwise stated. References in the text to authors' works are to books and articles which will be found in the Select Bibliography, grouped according to chapter.

The intention of the questions for discussion is to focus more clearly some of the issues I try to raise. My treatment of them has been deliberately provocative in places. I make no apology for this. I do not believe that genuine followers of Jesus need to be protected from the solid meat of God's revelation nor spoon-fed with what certain leaders think is a safe diet for them. The pretence that some subjects and opinions are either too difficult or too dangerous for the 'ordinary' Christian to handle is arrogant and paternalistic. I will be well satisfied if people tell me that they are either convinced or still remain sceptical about what I say, because at least they have tested the arguments against the Scriptures and their own experience of life. Please, no stereotyping!

Andrew Kirk, Harrow, April 1983

Introduction

No one can stand still

Surprising though it may seem, the most real thing about life for the Christian still lies ahead. Though based on solid historical facts of the past, and though needing to be applied in the present to every detail of life, Christian faith looks forward constantly to the end of history when God will make everything new again.

The early Christians, who either knew Jesus Christ personally or heard about him from those who did, expressed the importance of the future in a number of different ways. They used, for example, the story of Abraham as an illustration of how life should be understood. It is a journey whose ultimate destiny is certain. Along the route, however, nobody may settle down comfortably in the belief that they have already arrived.

Abraham and his family, like the modern bedouin, lived in tents. The essence of a tent is that it can be picked up, carried to somewhere else and pitched again in a short time. It allows one to be always on the move. A house, on the other hand, is a place to which one constantly returns. The house is an image of those who believe that the past is better than the present and who are afraid of the unknown qualities of the future.

Some Christians in the fifteenth century used to refer to the Church as the community of those who travel. In this way they expressed their conviction that all human life is moving towards a destiny in the future determined by the God 'who is, who was and who is to come'.

In fact, it is the story of Abraham in its deeper meaning that has altered the way most people today look at life. There used to be a time when people saw life in terms of a wheel that revolved endlessly without ever moving forward. Everyone was somewhere on that wheel, obliged to pass the same points again and again. This view was tied closely to the way people saw nature behaving. One season gave way to another. Year in and year out the same cycle was repeated. What happened this year would happen again next. The past would always be both the present and the future. People simply had no sense of history.

Abraham changed all that. Or rather, it was God who changed the way we see life. He promised Abraham that, as a result of a specific plan for the whole human race, his circumstances would alter dramatically. So Abraham left the changeless security of his home and set out for a new country and a new life.

Ever since that time we have gradually become used to thinking of life as a line that stretches from the past into the future, rather than as a circle with no past and no future.

But time is not limitless. For one thing, the universe will ultimately run out of energy. The Christian believes that God has set a limit to history as we now know it; though he cannot be certain about the timing of the end. He is certain, however, that at that time all violence, misuse of power, corruption, decay and suffering will be finished forever. God will bring in a new world marked by total harmony, reconciliation and justice, in which the worth and dignity of each individual is fully respected.

It is to this climax that history is moving. It is in the light of this future reality that the Christian must organise his whole life now. He is on a journey. If he is to travel with God, he should take no more than a tent with him; otherwise, he will discover that he has been left behind.

Facing the year 2000

The advent of a new millennium within the lifetime of most people alive today is a very special event. It presents a challenge to Christians to consider afresh how adequately they are expressing their faith to the real circumstances of today's world.

In a nutshell, that is what I will attempt to do in this book. Inevitably any one person has a limited and a biased point of view, so I cannot hope to do more than contribute some ideas to a discussion which, in the light of different experiences elsewhere, must go on throughout the whole Church.

The challenge does not come just because we are approaching a particular date. Nor does it arise only because changes in the world seem to occur at an increasingly bewildering speed. The Church presents its own kind of challenge to itself. There is a growing feeling, encountered all over the world, that the present dominant ways of seeing the Christian faith will no longer do. The faith has either become tangled up with a culture, language and structures which no longer release its power to be God's agent of new life and new hope, or else at crucial points it has been trimmed down to fit the beliefs of a world conditioned to reject all claims to final truth.

There is a malaise in the Church, a disenchantment with present ways of engaging the world with the gospel. Christians are looking for an authentic restatement of their faith which both adequately expresses the reality of the life they lead, and does justice to all that God has shown of himself in Jesus Christ. On close inspection it is amazing how many Christians base their understanding of the faith on traditions and beliefs that belong to a world which no longer exists. It does not matter much whether they call themselves conservative, radical or liberal; they have all made the mistake of allowing the faith to become identified with a particular passing view of reality. They have not seen that God's good news inevitably provokes disenchantment with all accepted beliefs and values, because it speaks to the present from the future.

It is my intention in these pages to try to respond to these challenges and to suggest some fresh ways of looking at the meaning of Christian faith. They will be critical of many cherished models being used at present.

I hope the book will be easy to read and follow. It is meant to be written in non-technical language in order to encourage a conversation among equals. Technical theological language is usually unnecessary, often irritating, and on many occasions a cover for a poor argument. I will therefore try to watch what I am saying.

Again, I want to resist the 'professional's' temptation to litter his pages with references to books and articles which mean little to most readers. Footnotes sometimes become an obsession, and their use may hide a certain degree of insecurity, alleviated by seeking to impress on others our high level of learning. In fact they betray a kind of thinking that springs more from discussion with the printed word than from reflection on the countless circumstances of ordinary life. Such a way of thinking depends upon a job that affords time to read and make notes on other people's books. Arguments should stand, or fall, on their own merits, irrespective of who may agree with them. I will, therefore, keep to a minimum my references. I have also made a list of books, to be found at the end, which I have found helpful, even though I may not necessarily agree with all they say.

Lopsided expressions of the faith

Some of the criticisms hinted at above about inadequate ways of expressing the Christian faith today need to be substantiated. I will look, therefore, at some of the current alternatives and discuss why I believe they are deficient.

(a) The evangelical

As my own Christian life has been moulded most closely by the tradition known as evangelical I will begin my misgivings as close to home as possible.

There are powerful currents in world evangelicalism which are pushing for what David Bosch (1980: 202f) calls an 'emaciated' gospel. The 1974 Lausanne Congress on World Evangelisation achieved a remarkable consensus among a broad cross-section of evangelical leaders from every corner of the globe. The Lausanne Covenant (Stott, 1975) painted in broad strokes the meaning of the gospel and the task of the Church. It did not avoid tackling certain controversial issues; for example: Christian social responsibility, the Church's captivity to culture, the disunity of evangelicals in evangelism and the need for affluent Christians to simplify their lifestyle. To many at Lausanne, and those who subsequently studied the document, the Covenant seemed to provide a new charter for the evangelical constitutency of the Church. It combined firmness about fundamental beliefs with humility, hope with repentance, trust in the power of the Spirit to renew the Church with a call to sacrificial living, acknowledgment of freedom in Christ with a call to responsible discipleship.

However, since Lausanne there has been a strong move in certain sections of the evangelical movement to interpret both the gospel and the task of the Church in much narrower terms. (I will return to an evaluation of this in greater detail in Chapter 8.) The Lausanne Committee for World Evangelisation (LCWE), founded at the 1974 Congress, convened a Consultation in Pattaya, Thailand, in June 1980. The purpose was threefold: to review the progress of world evangelisation since 1974; to produce reports and documents from seventeen mini-consultations giving ideas on how to reach different groups of people with the gospel (such as Buddhists, Marxists, the urban poor, nominal Roman Catholics and spiritists), and to discuss the future of the LCWE.

From the point of view of stimulating a greater faithfulness to the full biblical message of salvation in Jesus Christ, Pattaya was a great disappointment. From the beginning it was dominated by a group of people who represented the special interests of a certain sector of the North American evangelical world. This sector is characterised both by what it affirms and what it denies.

It affirms a view of evangelism linked to the theory of mission known as Church Growth. According to this view, evangelism is the verbal communication of a particular message in such a way that the number of converts to the Christian faith are maximised. Evangelisation, then, is a strategy that possesses a definite, measurable goal, a limited time-scale (the end of the century), and an efficient means of communication. The theme of Pattaya – '*How* shall they *hear*?' – emphasises this view. The tragedy of this 'emaciated' view of evangelism is not only that it conveniently ignores fundamental biblical teaching (as we shall see later), but that its proponents appear to be blind to its cultural roots in the Western economic tradition of free enterprise, pragmatism, success and organisational efficiency.

I believe that René Padilla's sharp analysis of the essential 'worldliness' of much Western evangelical Christianity (Douglas, 1975: 116–46) has not merely gone unheard, but has been deliberately ignored. The 'big business' of marketing and selling the gospel as efficiently as possible demands that the ends justify the means. The kind of defence-mechanism that has been set up to avoid the truth of the criticisms is at times ludicrous and at times sinister.

It is denied, for example, that all evangelism is inevitably linked to the political and social attitudes and activities of churches and individual Christians. At Pattaya a group of participants from Africa (including South Africa) produced a draft statement of concern drawing attention to the damage done to world evangelisation by evangelical leaders who support political and economic policies that deny the gospel. This eventually became a Statement of Concern on issues of social justice and their relation to world evangelisation. It was a short document (see Appendix) signed, within twenty-four hours, by about one-third of the participants. It was handed to Leighton Ford, the chairman of LCWE, with the request for guidelines on sociopolitical involvement in the light of the Lausanne Covenant (particularly sections 5 and 6), 'in order that World Evangelisation might be more credible and, therefore, more effective'.

The statement was received by the LCWE coolly and cautiously. A particular request to call another major consultation on social justice and its implications for world evangelisation was rejected.

More than anything else, this refusal to take seriously deep grassroots feelings has lessened the credibility of LCWE as a body that represents a wide cross-section of evangelical opinion.

My disenchantment with much contemporary evangelicalism springs ultimately from what I perceive to be a deep rift between its theory and its practice. Some North American evangelical leaders suggest that the crucial struggle for faithfulness in the coming years will concern the divine inspiration and inerrancy of the Scriptures (Lindsell, 1977; Chicago, 1978). Though personally I hold to a high view of Scripture, I do not see this as the crucial area for faithfulness. The 'battle' is not so much for one particular doctrine of the Bible as a struggle to discover and implement a right interpretation. Some evangelicals are notorious for the way they insist on the exact wording of doctrinal statements. At the same time, they are quite capable of ignoring or explaining away clear scriptural teaching on how to live. In particular we would mention the tendency to spiritualise concrete demands; to escape from the real world, through a highly speculative interpretation of prophecy, into a fantasy world of the future (e.g. Lindsey, 1971; Lindsey, 1973), and to separate the question of ends and means (e.g. in issues of war, violence and the use of wealth). Evangelicals cannot expect to be taken seriously by anyone else until they are much more honest and consistent in their use of the biblical text.

Other evangelicals maintain that the crucial issue before the Church today is the 'battle' for evangelism (Johnston, 1978). They accuse other Christians of abandoning commitment to evangelism, because they insist that active care for the poor and oppressed, leading to the need for some deep changes in the structures of society, is an essential part of discipleship. They believe that interest in social matters will automatically lessen commitment to evangelism and result in Christians becoming absorbed in secondary tasks (Hoekstra, 1979).

Such reasoning, however, lacks theological depth. It fails to ask seriously enough what the gospel is all about. The battle is not so much for evangelism as for the biblical gospel. The struggle is to discover how personal evangelism, social involvement, personal integrity, growth in the knowledge of God and in Christian fellowship can all be related together as indispensable parts of a total Christian witness.

Much of contemporary evangelicalism is perpetrating an unbiblical divorce between 'spiritual' salvation and liberation from evil structures and systems in the world. Pretending to be politically uncommitted, it shows itself to be deeply committed to its own brand of politics. Many of its present efforts are actually a hindrance to its stated aims of bringing the whole gospel to the whole man in the whole world. At the same time many of the current trends are a curious denial of the most solid theological and practical achievements of evangelicals in the past. In this book I will seek to recapture what seems to be of permanent value in the evangelical heritage as it relates to the challenges confronting the Church today.

(b) The liberal

Within the Church liberalism began to exert a strong influence from the beginning of the nineteenth century. It came largely from the secular tradition of the Enlightenment. It has, at some time, exercised a strong criticism of every imaginable belief and custom within the Church.

The movement has prided itself on its openmindedness. It has been ferociously critical of any claims to know the final truth about God, man and the universe, for it believes that such claims rest on the acceptance of dogma rather than on rigorous research. It has, therefore, been particularly sceptical about any final revelation of God in word and action. In practice, if not in theory, it has sat loosely to the biblical account of man's creation, fall and redemption in Christ. It has been characterised by an attitude to the Bible that assumes that the message is wrapped up in a view of the world largely at odds with the modern view. As a result, liberal Christians have given themselves the freedom to reinterpret any part of the Bible that does not seem to fit the modern world easily.

This last point takes us to the heart of the liberal way of looking at Christian faith. Its starting point is the accumulated wisdom of the modern, well educated mind. This is taken as a kind of standard to judge what may or may not be accepted from the Christian tradition of the past. The result has been a very considerable loss of confidence in the fundamental truths of the Christian faith as these have been believed and proclaimed since the time of the apostles. Among the articles of belief seriously questioned, drastically reinterpreted, or entirely scrapped are the pre-existence and virgin birth of Jesus Christ, the miracles he performed, his physical resurrection from death and ascension to heaven and his coming again to this world at the end of time. Many people in the liberal tradition have found the credal statement that Jesus of Nazareth was truly God impossible to accept.

A selective approach to the teaching of the Bible has also meant that the standards of the gospel on ethical issues such as abortion, homosexuality and relationships within and outside marriage have been relaxed in some Church circles.

However, the liberal approach to life and to the Christian faith is not as strong now as it has been in the past. It probably reached its peak of influence in the early 1960s. Since then it has declined in popularity and has been pushed on to the defensive. The whole approach has come under fire from three different quarters.

First, Christian liberalism has had a hard time reconciling its reinterpretation of belief with the clear meaning of basic Christian articles of faith inherited from the past. Put another way, it has not convinced either the majority of Church people or, for that matter, discerning and informed non-Christians, that there is much in common between the biblical statements and their recasting in modern forms of thought.

After a long and arduous attempt to convince the public, Christian and otherwise, that it is saying much the same thing as the authors of the Bible, the public remains sceptical. It remains stubbornly unconvinced, for example, that 'the ground of our being' is just another way of saying, 'Our Father in heaven'.

In other words, liberalism has a crisis of identity and integrity. The inner coherence between much of its thought and the fundamental beliefs of Christian faith, as the Church has always understood them, seem almost to have vanished. Liberalism may still be the guiding principle in some academic circles, but it has become marginal, in its old form, within the world Church as a whole.

Secondly, the pretence of liberalism to be based on an unprejudiced view of reality has now been strongly challenged. Many studies have been published in recent years showing how liberalism has tended to accept the basic assumptions of one particular, modern, intellectual tradition of the Western world.

Far from being a way of interpreting the Christian faith that starts from an undogmatic, objective view of human life in the contemporary world, it bases itself on a particular set of assumptions about the nature and scope of scientific investigation, the meaning of history and the way truth is discovered. Seeking to free itself from the bondage of a remote past, it has been held captive by a more recent past. Glorying in its critical judgment about everything else, it has failed to be critical about its own prejudices. In other words, liberalism has been exposed as the heir of a particular, biased, philosophical and cultural heritage. In the present clash of cultures, its limitations have become increasingly obvious. The intellectual heritage on which it is based is now seen to be just as dogmatic and intolerant as the heritage it tried to displace. Above all, the underlying idea that truth is discovered as a matter of historical progression within the civilisation that has given birth to the most democratic societies (i.e. Western Europe) is no longer tenable.

The liberal tradition undoubtedly possesses positive aspects, such as its refusal to accept beliefs and traditions merely on the authority of a ruling group in society or Church and its commitment to open investigation and discussion as the means to discovering how one should act today. Its weakness, however, lies in its apparent inability to acknowledge just how much it is a child of its times.

Thirdly, liberalism has been criticised for playing into the hands of certain ideological influences. In particular, Marxists and others have demonstrated that liberalism has, by its very nature, submitted to those forces in the Western world that seek to prevent any fundamental changes in the present economic and social balance of power.

Born in the age of Enlightenment, liberalism has cherished and promoted its ideals. However, belief in the inevitability of progress, the transforming power of scientific discovery and the ability of reason to overcome conflict has led liberalism into several impasses. It has tended to see change as a gradual, evolutionary strategy, a matter of two steps back and three steps forward. As a result, liberalism has been incapable of mounting a coherent, alternative vision of society. It sails in the same boat as those whose interests demand that the old model be kept intact.

Moreover, as has been demonstrated in places like South Africa, the inner cities of Britain and the USA, and the Middle East, liberalism as a view of human life has shown itself incapable of handling areas of conflict. Its dislike of dogmatism means that it finds it hard to get to grips with issues of justice, violence and radical change.

In an age of revolution liberalism is out of date. Its set of assumptions will not stand up to the rigours of tomorrow's world. The call is to work out now a consistent system of values and beliefs capable of meeting the challenge of apocalyptic times.

(c) The radical
Since the mid-1960s revolution rather than evolution has seemed to many Christians the only way of achieving a society more in conformity with the spirit of Christ. Radical action rather than comforting

platitudes is being demanded by increasing numbers of people outside the Western world. Liberal economics and social reform has proved itself ineffective in bringing real, substantial development to the mass of humanity caught in the downward spiral of acute deprivation. Tinkering with the mechanics of the system is a totally inadequate response to the real needs of the majority of humanity. Only an entirely new engine will do.

In Christian circles nowhere has this demand for a drastic, revolutionary shift of power and resources to the poor been more cogently argued and more insistently proclaimed than by a strong sector in the World Council of Churches (WCC).

At least since 1966 a steady flow of books and study documents, of manpower and financial gifts, have come forth from Geneva. They commend and seek to implement the WCC's call for radical political, social and economic measures to help end a world where the division between the wealthy and the deprived is structured by the way the systems work.

Today one can talk about a new kind of ecumenism. Irritated and frustrated by the time consumed on talks and schemes for Church union, it advocates the unity of broken humanity as of first priority. Unity is not seen as the reconciliation of differing viewpoints in which all sides agree to modify their claims, for in a world where power is not equally shared one group can dictate the terms of peace to the other. Rather, unity is seen as the end-product of a period of intense conflict in which the powerless win back for themselves the inalienable rights of equality and self-determination which have been withheld from them.

The radical Christian (particularly in liberation, black and feminist theology) interprets the faith of the Bible almost exclusively in terms of the struggle for a new kind of society. As he sees the tide of totalitarianism creep steadily up the beach, he becomes increasingly convinced that a Church committed unreservedly to the poor, and to the God who became poor and by suffering triumphed over all the forces of privilege and oppression, is the only body left with the resilience and motivation to effect the far-reaching changes needed.

The radical, however, in his highly commendable emphasis on the needs and rights of the deprived peoples, on social justice and an end to oppression and exploitation has, like the evangelical and liberal, become unbalanced in his understanding of the message of the Bible. He also shows an inadequate appreciation of the subtle way that human sin works its way out in society.

Radical Christians have over-reacted to the narrow individualism of the Western world. In their stress on the corporate and structural nature of evil they have failed to do justice to the individual nature of human guilt and lostness. As a result they have underestimated the destructive quality of sin in all people. They have emphasised too much the influence of circumstances upon acts of injustice and violence.

One popular, current view of liberation does not, therefore, take sufficiently seriously the poisonous nature of sin in the human mind. The radical solution to global oppression – revolution from below – assumes that the poor are more sinned against than sinners, and that freedom is a process achieved by a greater awareness of the causes of one's social circumstances.

In line with this inadequate view of the reality of human nature is the understanding of the meaning of Christ's sacrifice for sin. The crucifixion is interpreted largely in terms of the death of a prophet at the hands of callous, self-seeking wielders of political privilege. It is seen as the result of an unparalleled identification by Jesus with the oppressed of his time. This, in my opinion, *is* a correct reading of what happened to Jesus. However, the fact that Jesus died for every person, because we are all enemies of God, is largely absent. The cross as God's response to the curse of original sin under which everyone lives is ignored.

The radical tends, therefore, to issue a discriminating call to repentance and conversion. Sometimes he gives the impression that the oppressed and those who act in solidarity with them are saved by their (unselfish) commitment to the struggle for a better kind of existence: they liberate themselves from submission to a tyrannical system of power and they liberate the exploiters by helping them to see how they are accomplices to injustice.

Finally, the radical is inclined to believe that a different economic order will solve the majority of the most pressing and stubborn problems affecting human society. I heard an Indian university lecturer arguing passionately that unemployment was almost unknown in socialist societies. He did not show so much as a flicker of recognition of the possibility that full employment was achieved either by the massive expulsion of people from the territory (as in Cuba or Vietnam) or by maintaining an excessively large standing army (as in Russia). A correct criticism of one economic system (capitalism) does not automatically imply the rightness of that system which historically has been opposed to it (socialism). Neither has begun to achieve what it has promised. Both have to be made to work in a society of real people with a natural inclination to maximise their own interests. To pretend that human beings outside of new life in Christ, are not self-seeking is to fly in the face of facts that have been accumulating for thousands of years.

The radical, like the liberal and evangelical Christian, has selected those parts of the biblical message he is prepared to accept. As a result his diagnosis of the human condition is not radical enough. His cure only deals with the symptoms, serious though they are.

In this brief description of some ways in which Christians are interpreting their core beliefs today I am aware of the danger of over-simplification. With more space one would probably make some qualifications. Nevertheless, the three groups I have touched on see themselves as distinct from one another, and at times quite strongly opposed. In theory they might want to refine the way in which others see them; in practice they have left their distinctive mark by emphasising only a part of God's message to the world.

The differences noted above have little to do with the separation of Christian denominations. Most of the serious disagreements among Christians today transcend the boundaries of denominations. This is not to deny that some Churches are, in their official position, more closely identified with the teaching of the Bible than others. It means either that all official doctrinal statements are insufficient, or at places in error, or that individuals or groups of Christians pay little heed to what their denominations say.

Signs of an alternative

To accuse other people of having a lopsided view implies that one believes that there is an alternative way of understanding God's message within the complexities of life today. One assumes that it is possible to retain the best of each view and to discard misplaced ideas.

This is not a theoretical judgment. Already here and there, particularly among some Christians in the Third World, we may discern evidence of a fresh and relevant grasp of the implications of following Jesus Christ. A new openness both to the offer and the demands of the gospel is to be found among the urban poor and those identified with their plight; among a variety of intentional communities; among those engaged in programmes of theological renewal and the transformation of theological training; among those experimenting in a new Christian approach in the arts; among those willing to sacrifice reputation, employment, freedom, and even life itself to stand against racism, social injustice, nationalistic bigotry and violence; among those confronted with the need to find new ways of making Jesus credible to people of other faiths.

These groups may not appear to have much in common. Yet, I believe, a new consensus about the scope and meaning of the gospel is on the horizon. It may still show marks of ambiguity. In some respects it may be hesitant and tentative. Underneath, however, a kind of theological coherence is beginning to take shape. I want to try to spell out the boundaries of this consensus in this book.

Of course, I shall give my own interpretation of it. That is inevitable. Others may want to stress other elements, or to disagree with details here and there. I hope they will be stimulated to explain carefully and graciously where and why they disagree. I have organised my understanding of the new consensus in three areas: the centrality of the theme of the kingdom in God's message for the world; response to the poor of the earth; and the task of evangelism. At the end I offer some suggestions about how the Church needs to look if it is going to respond faithfully to the calling of its Lord to live and communicate his gospel. But first we should look again at the kind of world our generation has been destined to live in.

1: The glories and follies of a passing age

A momentous year

Historical movements never have an exact beginning, nor end. Their origins are never single, but multiple. Their demise can be likened not so much to a car written off after a serious crash but to an old 'banger' which fails its test once too often. We cannot date them, therefore, with the precision of, say, the German invasion of Russia in 1941, or the final of the World Cup in Spain in 1982.

Nevertheless, it is possible to detect important historical landmarks. Some events clearly exercise a far greater influence on the subsequent course of history than others. In this sense, for two important reasons, the modern era may be said to have begun in 1776. In that year the colonies of North America won their independence from British rule. The peoples of the Eastern seaboard set out on the path that took them to becoming 'top nation'.

The consequences of this event were to have a profound effect on the course of world history (as shrewd observers, like Karl Marx, were swift to perceive), not least on the expansion of Christian faith across the world. From that time on, the characteristic North American doctrine of 'manifest destiny' (the sense of being a people divinely chosen and equipped to lead, guide and convert the whole world) gathered momentum.

In the same year Adam Smith published his celebrated tract on economics, *Nature and Causes of the Wealth of Nations*. In the words of Daniel Fusfield (1972: 5), his argument gave a new lease of life to 'the proposition that a private enterprise economy tends to maximize individual welfare'. The importance of Smith's work lies in its symbolic value as the theoretical foundation for the capitalist system of production and distribution, and the particular values of economic growth and consumerism it enshrines.

American independence and the growth of free-enterprise capitalism are strongly linked. Together their efforts have penetrated the remotest corners of the globe. Goods 'made in Taiwan,' or 'made in Korea' are a direct result of events that happened more than 200 years ago. These events continue to do more to shape the kind of world we live in and the problems we face than any other comparable event during that period.

Characteristics of the modern age

The pattern of our daily lives, many of the assumptions we take for granted about our existence, and a number of the values we have adopted are the direct outcome of a free-enterprise economy. Even Marxism, an influential political ideology since the late nineteenth century, is in some ways no more than a reaction to Adam Smith and the growth of British economic theory and practice.

When sociologists describe the basic characteristics of the modern age (sometimes called 'modernity' for short) they are talking about a number of different things. In general they are referring to an entire way of life backed up by a set of beliefs about the meaning of goodness and truth. It is a kind of cultural atmosphere that we breathe at home, at school and via contact with the mass media. These beliefs have formed the habits and lifestyle of the vast majority of the populations of industralised nations. Christians, often, are no exception.

The assumptions of the modern age, not usually seriously questioned today, have been listed by Thomas Ogden in his book, *Agenda for Theology* (1979: xii). He speaks of autonomous individualism, secularisation, anti-supernaturalism and the pursuit of pleasure as an end in itself. He characterises the modern world, above all, as one that puts its faith in all things new: 'which assumes that recent modes of knowing the truth are vastly superior to older ways'. We might call this belief the evolutionist fallacy: the notion that the passing of time itself brings a certain progress and that a qualitative leap into a better future is certain to be around the next corner.

Such a view is substantiated in the minds of some by the fact that it claims to be based on good scientific data. However, it is precisely the need to invest science and scientists with an aura of unquestioned authority that is a mark of the modern age. In contrast to the purveyors of religion who are the medicine-men of the past and the politicians who are dangerous amateurs in a game too tough for them, scientists are the real professionals.

The intellectual developments of the last 200 years have been made possible by the extraordinary economic growth of this period. Among other things the growth has made possible an unprecedented expansion of education. It has also allowed considerable funds to be made available for scientific research.

Partly as a result of this we have witnessed the curious anomaly of C. P. Snow's two cultures. On the one hand, we find an optimistic view of the world that suggests that mankind, through the progressive control of his environment, has reached the threshold of a new era. On the other hand, we get drawn into an artistic world plunged into pessimism and bewilderment. Now one side, now the other, seems to sway our judgment of what the future holds.

Whatever we feel about humanity's intellectual achievements, doubts, arrogance or sheer boredom, there is no doubt that the economic context of its life becomes more crucial every day. Whether we think that free-enterprise capitalism has been mainly beneficial, mostly disastrous, or perhaps a mixed blessing, its assumption that the main purpose of man's life is the pursuit of happiness to be achieved by the constant expansion of goods and services is the basis of our daily political and economic life. Whether we consider that we are well off or struggling to make ends meet the attainment of a better standard of living is the constant goal of most people. Even in areas of the world where the majority have no chance of rising much above the poverty line, an affluent lifestyle, available only to small groups of privileged people, beckons from advertisements and shop windows.

Affluence is the result of what Engels called the greatest revolution of all time – the progressive control and management through applied science of natural resources in the interests of mankind's physical well-being. The last 250 years have certainly witnessed a number of staggering achievements. Discoveries in medical science, in particular, have meant that life itself is less open to chance. Most people in so-called developed countries expect to enjoy a normal, healthy existence until well into their sixties, or seventies.

Without cataloguing in detail all the benefits that increased rational knowledge of the physical world has brought, one can sum it up by saying that life today has considerable more variety about it than in the past. What technological advance does is greatly expand the number of choices open to us. In this sense man has much greater freedom than his ancestors had. One obvious example of this is the freedom to visit parts of the world which previously would have been inaccessible to all but the most intrepid explorers.

And even they would not have been able to visit several different continents within the same week or month. Air travel and modern communications have caused both time and space to shrink. In forty years peoples, previously living a stone-age existence in the interior of New Guinea, can experience travel by jet and enjoy a university education in Port Moresby, Melbourne or San Francisco.

It is this kind of freedom from physical constraint and necessity that has been such an important feature of the modern age. The apparently endless possibilities of pushing the frontiers of scientific experiment outwards lends to life a certain exhilaration and hope.

However, both the achievements and the sense of power and control over our environment that they give also dull our ability to look critically at the dark side of the kind of society we have created.

The economic system (capitalism) that determines to a large degree the kind of life we live began to flower in the latter part of the eighteenth century. There have been two major explanations of its origin. Marx believed, and sought to demonstrate by means of historical analysis, that a certain pattern of wealth-creation when developed to a particular point would give birth to a society divided into wealth-owners (capitalists or bourgeoisie) and wealth-creators (workers or proletariat). From the thirteenth century onwards a relentless struggle took place in Europe between the expanding merchant class and the ancient nobility. It was only a matter of time before the feudal society was doomed to disappear. Marx's explanation of the rise of capitalism concentrates on the relationship between economic forces and changes in technological achievement. That is why it is called a materialist view.

Weber believed that uninhibited accumulation of wealth and the creation of capital needed some kind of ethical or philosophical justification. He found it in the view of work that was put forward by the leaders of the Reformation. Work was seen, not as a result of God's curse on the human race, but rather as a divine calling, a mandate from God himself to fulfil. Work was instituted by God as the proper means of providing for the necessities both of the family unit and those unable to work. To subdue the earth was one of the chief ways of glorifying the Creator. A strong emphasis, particularly among Puritan Christians, on a simple and sober lifestyle made saving and investment possible. Weber's theory has been called idealist because of its emphasis on the religious context of the rise of capitalism.

Both theories, in my opinion, are part of a correct explanation. However, some of the deductions often made from them need to be challenged. Some Christians have assumed that the so-called 'Protestant Work Ethic' gives a biblical sanction to the capitalist system as such. Such a view, however, is based on much confusion.

As capitalist economic theory and practice progressed the principal values on which it operated soon became divorced from the Reformation view of God and man. It has been strongly maintained, for example, that each individual's pursuit of economic self-interest will ultimately benefit everyone else. The absolute sanctity of private property is also a cornerstone of the system. Its justification, however, is based on the delusion that personal wealth is always accumulated by fair and honest means. Religious and civil freedom has been linked closely with economic free enterprise, as if there was some necessary connection between them. Even the doctrine of original sin has been enlisted as an argument for capitalist economics. It is suggested that in a selfish world the only incentive to work is necessarily a good material return on the energy expended, that is, the motive of profit.

Finally, capitalism became infused with the philosophy of the Enlightenment. Its massive retreat from the discipline of God's Word has led, among other things, to an intense individualism based on the view that people must be free to do what they want as long as their freedom does not restrict that of others to pursue the same ends. The result of a literally Godless concept of man has been an economy in which achievement is measured by those fittest enough (or ruthless enough) to survive. Without strict legal controls the market-place soon degenerates into the jungle.

Moreover capitalism is dependent on an expanding market, on sustained growth. It has cleverly and systematically exploited the Enlightenment notion of man's chief end being the pursuit of his own happiness. In a free-market economy resources are allocated on the basis of supply and demand. Production is dependent on the demand for an object. But demands can be artificially stimulated. As real human needs are limited, but wants are infinite, there is plenty of scope for powerful advertising to persuade us that our wants are really needs.

The result of this process may lead ultimately to the demise of capitalism. There are a number of economists who believe that capitalism, by its very success (in its own terms), destroys itself. For example, the original goal of work, and even of production, has now largely been replaced by the goal of consumption. This tends to create a mentality among all sections of the population, irrespective of the class to which each belongs, which seeks to achieve for oneself a maximum buying-power for a minimum input. The work ethic has been transformed into the consumer ethic. Work is identified with employment and employment with financial reward. An ethic of pure consumerism cannot sustain an expanding economy based on high output and low wages. Marx used the word fetishism to describe the process. The biblical prophets would have called it covetousness, which is idolatry. We will return to a critique of capitalism in Part Three.

If some Christians have thrown in their lot uncritically with a market economy, others have accepted Marx's critique of it without question and identified the Faith with some brand of socialism.

Marx has been accused of inventing a new economic structure whose results would reverse most of the gains of a free-enterprise system. His actual views, however, have become confused in some peoples' minds because of their identification with the Stalinist model of a command economy. Marx's ideas have been defended by some Christians on the grounds that he rediscovered the prophetic message of the Bible in its application to economic affairs.

Because the words of Jesus 'your heart will always be where your riches are' are true, the subject of economics engenders enormous passions. Marx himself rarely gets a fair hearing either from his detractors or his venerators. His greatest achievement, in fact, was to examine and identify the ways in which the capitalist system worked. Of course, his analysis was not free of value judgments and interpretation. However, he himself did not invent the class struggle nor the concept of surplus-value. He simply gave the names to what already existed as an integral part of the system. He converted a reality that was easily observable into a theory of production relations. It seems to me that as a piece of sound economic analysis this part of his theory is still largely valid. The capitalist system, by its very nature, is predatory: one class uses another to its own financial ends.

Where Marx and his followers have gone sadly wrong is in believing they can predict the future course that capitalism must take. They fail to convince. Even if the recurring crises of capitalism eventually lead to its breakdown and replacement by a new way of ordering economic life, there is no absolute certainty that we will have arrived at a socialism in which the division between the owners and producers of wealth is finally, for all time, finished. The Marxist confidence in the outcome of history is, in its blindness, almost superstitious.

Marx was, like his contemporaries, a child of the Enlightenment.

He suffered as a result from at least two influences that he never seriously examined. He believed, first, that history was developing towards the resolution of all conflicts. Unlike the philosopher Hegel, he thought this would be achieved by material rather than spiritual progression. Secondly, he shared the romantic belief about primitive societies that they were less alienated in their human relations than all subsequent ones. He believed that the primitive ideal of a harmonious society could be re-established in the future even within a much more complex human community. This was his vision of a communist state.

He never explained, nor have any of his followers, why new forms of class division should not replace existing ones. Marx and Engels repudiated any and every form of Utopianism. Their followers, however, have been forced to use various forms of coercion to bring about this romantic notion of a communist society.

Both capitalism and Marxism, then, are but different expressions of the follies of the modern age. They are products of Western man's striving for freedom and his equation of this with mastery of the environment. Capitalism has exalted the freedom of the individual to pursue his own self-interests. It has not been able, however, to find a way of achieving this without promoting considerable financial discrimination. The result has been the loss of freedom for many others. Marxism has exalted collective freedom – the freedom of everyone to enjoy a basically dignified life – but it has achieved this only by imposing a rigid ideological conformity and control on the whole of society. The result has also been the loss of freedom of many to be humanly creative and to express dissent.

There is another factor about the modern age that only recently has received much notice and that is the historical and cultural self-centredness of European civilisation. Capitalism and Marxism are both products of this ethnocentricity. Experiments, such as African socialism, are laughed to scorn as belonging to an underdeveloped situation and mentality.

However, the smile may be on the other side of the tiger's face. The West (including the European East) is clearly in the midst of a crisis. It is true that the present order may not be in any imminent likelihood of collapsing. There is still some resilience left. Nevertheless, the West is not achieving its own goals. Freedom is as elusive as it was 200 years ago. As long as there was an upward spiral of economic progress an illusion of development towards a fuller kind of life has been given. Access to an increasing quantity of life (goods and services) has postponed the debate (which economic theory, based on a view of man with God left out, cannot in any case answer) about its quality.

When men and women can no longer fulfil the purpose in life that the culture has invented for them – the pursuit of happiness through the possession of things – a new basic goal must be manufactured. Here our discussion brings us full circle, for affluence has dulled our sensibilities. We now find it almost impossible to conceive of a different kind of life, stripped of the clutter of trivialities and waste.

As far as the Church is concerned it has in many instances adopted structures, strategies and goals that prevent it from seeing how far it has moved away from the essential values of the gospel. It has been so in debt to the system, so personally committed to its success, that it has failed to achieve for itself that freedom in Christ which is at the very heart of its message.

In biblical terms there is no such thing as 'spiritual' freedom while people are still held captive by a form of life that contradicts the mind of Christ. Conversion, about which Christians sometimes speak rather glibly, involves much more than turning away from individual acts of selfishness, self-indulgence and violence. It means embracing wholeheartedly the kingdom of God and its righteousness. There are some signs that this kind of conversion is on the way in the Church in the West, though there is still much resistance. We will explore the implications of this conversion in more detail in Part Two. First we will complete our picture of this age by looking at possible trends for the future.

2: Signs of panic and signs of hope

Chickens coming home to roost

The appalling possibility of a nuclear holocaust with its literally devastating outcome is beginning to shake the consciousness of Europe today. The now celebrated lines, 'the turtles that are left will wear human-neck sweaters', are quoted not just with a wry smile but with some idea that their fulfilment could be more than a sick joke.

Western nations, as we have already suggested, have become accustomed to thinking of themselves as the centre of the world. However, their vaunted civilisation and achievements are in peril of death and destruction through radiation. If political propaganda continues to insist that the main characteristic of our world is the struggle between the Russian bear and the American eagle then Europe will bear the brunt of any conflict that cannot be contained within diplomatic negotiation. Even if war could be contained within a limited geographical area (is the technical language of a 'theatre' a reference to the most mammoth spectacle ever staged, or to a clinical post-mortem examination?), millions would probably die a painful death, further millions would be mutilated for life or suffer irreparable psychological damage, the industrial base of highly sophisticated societies would be destroyed and famous monuments like the Coliseum, St Mark's, Venice, the Louvre and Canterbury Cathedral would crumble away to nothing.

Europe, of course, has lived with this kind of threat for over three decades. Some will be tempted to say that if hostilities are going to break out, they would have done so long ago. Europe has managed to survive a number of crises over this period. The art of diplomacy is to know how to go to the brink and then step back.

Nevertheless, there are some new factors in the situation that are producing increasing signs of alarm, if not yet of outright panic. First, the capability for mutual annihilation was passed many years ago. Yet the increase in nuclear arms of aggression continues unabated. The two sides have given plenty of evidence that they are incapable of agreeing to and carrying out any meaningful reduction of arms. As a result, ordinary people when they contemplate the so-called arms-limitation negotiations are inclined to believe that a steady build-up of arms may become a self-fulfilling prophecy. The history of previous wars suggests that the outbreak of violence was immediately preceded by an unusually large build-up of arms. Secondly, the public has begun to think for itself, rather than to accept meekly the monotonous chanting of the deterrence lobby. Many more people than previously have begun to question the assumptions and the logic of nuclear defence.

The debate is complex, highly charged and very contemporary. It would be foolish of me even to begin to try to unravel the strengths and weaknesses of the arguments on both sides. This is not my immediate purpose. Rather, I want to use the question of nuclear warfare as an instance of the kind of world to which the gospel of Jesus must be addressed with meaning and with power.

The thesis of this chapter is that the potential for panic aroused by the vision of a nuclear holocaust can best be understood as the chickens of Western aggression coming home to roost. At the same time the gravity of the situation is giving rise to hope that the Western world may substantially reconsider its own history and present role in the world.

A new version of history

The peoples of Africa, Asia and Latin America have gained a new self-consciousness in the last thirty years and a new influence in world affairs. This has led them to develop accounts of historical development over the last millenium quite distinct from those found in the textbooks of the West. It is all a matter of perspective.

Most of the so-called Third World nations have been subject to colonisation from the West. Armies, traders and civil servants have taken over huge territories by force and have governed them according to the policies, laws and customs of countries geographically and culturally remote. The invaders have not held themselves accountable to local people. Rather, they have served first the interests of those who sent them.

It is not surprising, therefore, that former colonies now interpret the history of the West in terms of repeated and sustained acts of aggression. When seen from the situation of peoples who have suffered, against their will, the ambition and greed of European power the world looks very different.

Third World peoples view themselves as living on the periphery of history. Their existence is governed by decisions taken by nations who have made themselves militarily and economically powerful and well-nigh invulnerable. They live, therefore, as if on the outer edge of a giant wheel, driven from a geographically distant centre, which spins on aimlessly into the future. As technology 'advances' the wheel spins faster, but those on the circumference experience the strange sensation of going backwards.

Colonialism, save in a very few cases, is no longer felt as the physical presence of foreign troops. Today it is experienced in the highly genteel and civilised spectacle of smartly groomed executives from the World Bank, the International Monetary Fund and foreign companies stepping from aeroplanes and being driven to the local Hilton to negotiate financial arrangements with local governments. In Malaysia today it is said that Japan has achieved commercially what it could not bring about by military means – domination of the economic life of the country.

Physical aggression, however, is not far below the surface, if needed. Maximum productive efficiency and control of world commerce by Western companies requires political stability and ideological compatibility. As recent history has abundantly illustrated, organised opposition to the economic policies of international capitalism (or in the cases of Poland, Kampuchea and Afghanistan, opposition to Russian socialism) have been met with severe, systematic repression. The cost of maintaining the present international order on the road is absolutely devastating: martial law, arrest without trial, torture, genocide, abductions and cold-blooded murders, deteriorating physical conditions for hundreds of millions (nourishment, health and shelter) and the devastation of the earth's natural life (the rape of the forests, in Brazil, Nepal and Malaysia, for example).

Since 1980 the situation of Poland has been in the forefront of Western concern. For particular historical reasons Poland has a special place in the consciousness of Western nations. The struggle there by ordinary citizens for a real say in the management of their country is desperately important. For a time it looked as if, for the first time, a mass movement in a socialist state had a chance of effecting a more democratic society. Now, for some time at least, it may be the last.

It has been reported that Western governments and their advisers were genuinely surprised that the crack-down on Solidarity came from within Poland, rather than by Warsaw Pact forces from without. If the report is true it shows an extraordinary inability to see that events in Poland resemble closely those in countries in which Western nations have a direct influence. North American foreign policy, for example, is possibly a little more sophisticated than it was in the days of 1965 when the marines were ordered into Santo Domingo. The USA may even have learnt something from the débâcle of Vietnam. So, Western interests today in the Third World are best served by indirect involvement, by supporting through diplomatic, military and financial means governments (often military dictatorships far more ruthless than the regime of General Jaruzelski) who can be relied on to guarantee that no fundamental change will take place.

The hidden aggression of the West in supporting totalitarian governments of the nature of Turkey, Chile, El Salvador, South Korea, the Philippines and Pakistan has made many people dismally blind to the sheer hypocrisy of their outrage over Poland. On 1st February, 1982 the American Secretary of State is reported to have stated that 'there is a spirit of Solidarity in the world which no physical force can crush'. He is precisely right, but such a spirit applies not only to Mr Walesa and his colleagues, but to peasants in Guatemala; the mothers of the disappeared who (until the coming of a democratically elected government in December 1983) stood forlornly every Thursday in the Plaza de Mayo in Buenos Aires; tin-miners in Bolivia; civic leaders in Soweto; those under house arrest or in gaol in scores of countries for daring to resist a consistent, flagrant violation of human rights. Mr Haig is right, the spirit exists wherever men, women and children refuse to be crushed by the long-arm of Western (including Soviet) aggression.

Aggression in personal terms: the case of abortion

The aggressive instincts so much in evidence in the colonial and economic expansion of Europe are evident today in less obvious ways. At the level of family units and individuals there is abroad a spirit of self-assertion that manifests itself in a particular attitude to personal lifestyle. In discussing such highly controversial issues as divorce, abortion and pornography, I think it is vital that we see them as part of the same self-indulgent drive as has caused the present Western opposition to a real global, political and economic partnership.

Perhaps we could best sum up the attitude as a relentless determination to pursue my own individual rights. It has now become a deeply embedded belief in Western culture that the individual has the right to pursue his or her own inclinations freely. In those matters generally considered to be part of a person's private world, the law, it is strongly stated, should not interfere to restrict choice. The right of abortion, for example, is defended, by those who believe it is basically a question of a mother's choice, as a matter of individual freedom.

It is interesting to see how keen pro-abortionists are to take debate out of the public arena. Medical practitioners are made the arbiters of when to terminate the beginning of human life. However, there is a fatal flaw in this process. Doctors, as such, are not qualified to decide the really basic issues. First, it is beyond the scope of medical science to define the meaning, and therefore the beginning, of human life. Arguments about the number of weeks before which an abortion may be permissible are irrelevant. Even if a foetus cannot survive outside the womb before a certain period, it simply means the foetus needs that kind of environment to go on living. Secondly, doctors are not qualified by themselves to decide under what social conditions the mother would be justified in having an abortion. Thirdly, a doctor is not in a position to define the potential quality of life of a deformed foetus. One wonders whether the authority given to doctors in this matter is not yet another example of contemporary society needing to invest science with the power to arbitrate over questions literally of life and death. There is, of course, a perfectly legitimate area of competence for doctors to decide: that of serious health hazards to the mother.

The debate about abortion refuses to go away. It can never be confined to a decision taken by a doctor in private consultation with the mother. It is essentially an ethical issue: to do with a society's perception of what it means to be human. Abortion on demand tells us about society's aggressive instincts. Laws that allow this to happen, do not lessen the underlying aggression by being called 'liberal'.

Whether or not a pregnancy is considered 'wanted' is a matter of the climate of opinion in a given society. 'Unwanted' can be induced by suggestion and then strengthened by making the suggestion legally possible. Many other societies operate on the premise that 'unwanted' in the case of embryonic life is not an option.

It is clear from the intense debate of two decades that legalised abortion is seen by some as a triumph of individual liberty, as a victory of individual rights against the coercive power of the state. In one way this is true. However, the deeper questions concerning freedom and rights is seldom dealt with. There is a direct parallel with the freedom claimed for a free-enterprise economic system.

One person's freedom may be another's lack of freedom. Abortion has been discussed too much in terms of the individual's rights. This is precisely what we would expect in an aggressive culture. Little attention is paid to the consequences of these so-called rights. There is, in fact, a considerable cost to be born.

One needs to consider, for example, the loss of opportunity to provide real care which more-or-less instant abortion takes away. One instance of this is the kind of loving counselling and support that can convert the 'unwanted' into the wanted; another, the heroic acts of self-sacrificial love by those parents and others who have dedicated themselves to care for mongol, spinabifida and other handicapped children. In spite of the tragedy of such children, it could well be argued that the moral strength of the people who lavish a loving devotion upon them has been exalted. Thirdly, there is the possibility of adoption. On one side many parents, unable to have children themselves and unable to find children for adoption, are frustrated. On the other side, caring for babies in a situation where the natural parents cannot cope gives deep satisfaction. Lack of babies increases frustration and diminishes satisfaction.

There are strong reasons for arguing that abortion-on-demand is a reversion to a more primitive stage of civilisation where the unusual and the unnatural cannot be allowed in public view. We find ourselves once again embarrassed and ashamed to deal with the chronically unhealthy. Elimination of such babies, however, would decrease rather than enhance the reality of a so-called caring society. Is not the argument that we cannot cope a sign of panic? And is not aggression a typical response to panic?

So far, we have deliberately not used specifically Christian arguments in the debate about abortion. However, they too are highly relevant. The Christian view on rights is determined by the relationship of the individual to the exercise of power in society. The rights to be defended and extended are those of the least powerful. They are the ones whose rights are violated by others, more powerful, insisting on their rights. This view springs from the fact that God begins here: 'He protects the strangers who live in our land; he helps widows and orphans' (Ps. 146.9). What life is more helpless and vulnerable than that of an unborn child? Yet 'when my bones were being formed, carefully put together in my mother's womb, when I was growing there in secret, you know that I was there – you saw me before I was born' (Ps. 139.15–16).

Irresponsible access to abortion is as clear an example of the individualistic self-assertion of Western society as is the present world economic order. They may appear to be widely different issues. Yet, I believe, they are all of a piece. The reader can reflect for himself or herself how other matters such as divorce, on the grounds of the breakdown of a marriage, and pornography, as a commercial venture, are further examples of individualistic aggression and the abuse of freedom.

The struggle against aggression

The survival of the human race as such depends on curbing the aggression that goes into the arms race. The survival of a dignified life depends on curbing the aggression that violates the rights of the powerless. Are there any signs of hope that humanity, the Western nations in particular, are learning these lessons?

One sign, I believe, is that arguments are being more publicly aired. Often they are leading to non-violent tactics to bring a change of direction. Let us look at two controversial examples.

(a) Deterrence and disarmament

Everyone believes in disarmament, but those who favour multilateral treaties have little to show for their convictions. The growing response to demonstrations and lobbying in favour of arms reductions, whether or not they are matched by the other side, is based on a series of significant arguments.

First, the alternative strategy of negotiated deals between nuclear powers seems to have reached an impasse. Any initiative to break the deadlock, to be genuinely new, must begin with actions rather than words. Words are relatively safe; actions are part of a calculated risk to bring a new situation into being.

Secondly, the strategy of nuclear deterrence is based exclusively on a massive bluff. To fulfil its function the potential aggressor has to believe that the opponent will retaliate in kind. And yet, strategically and politically nothing can be gained from firing back once one's own country and population has been decimated. Even a counterstroke, let alone a first use, is, in effect, quite indefensible from any point of view save that of naked revenge.

Thirdly, there is a growing awareness that the logic of the cold war springs from two basic, questionable assumptions. First, Russia is the chief enemy. Secondly, if Western powers abolished the means of nuclear reprisal, Russia would automatically take the opportunity to annex the nations of Western Europe. One wonders, though, whether the case of Finland and Yugoslavia are exceptions that prove the rule. One also wonders what changes might be effected in Russia, if she began to be treated less as the source of all evil. For a Christian there is the added consideration that the majority of Russians claim to belong to Jesus Christ. Is indiscriminate killing of fellow citizens of the new age a consistent way for Christians to behave?

Fourthly, building up nuclear capability is a clear way of demonstrating that confidence in the moral and cultural resilience of the West is lacking. There is no expectation, apparently, that the peoples of Western Europe could resist the imposition of an alien regime other than by being prepared to administer instant death to millions of innocent people. If this is the case, where is the superiority of Western European moral values? Maybe the military establishment is right about Russian intentions? If so, then what kind of a society are the nuclear warheads supposed to be defending? The freedom of a culture to erode its moral resolve even further? It could certainly be interpreted in this way.

The importance of these arguments does not lie in the fact that they are totally irrefutable – the issues are too complex and the stakes too high for any easy answers – but that they demonstrate a new mood. We can detect, by a willingness to become vulnerable, an attempt to break new ground. Such a gesture would be the opposite of aggression, for the latter seeks to find its security in holding the balance of power. Vulnerability, on the other hand, exposes one to the uncertainty of how the other side might react. As such it is a calculated action to limit one's physical power, the very opposite of panic. Nevertheless, without a confidence firmly rooted in an active God it is unlikely that this particular sign of hope will sustain itself for long.

(b) Development aid

In the field of development there are also some signs that Western economic aggression may give way to a new spirit of partnership. As in the case of nuclear deterrence, the signs come from within society rather than from those in positions of power at the top.

Within the last twenty years or so there has been an enormous increase in the number and scale of Western aid and development agencies. They have made, and continue to make, mistakes. Sometimes the finance made available is attached to conditions that enhance the power and prestige of the donor. Nevertheless, little by little, many agencies are transferring resources – of people, skills, technology and money – in a way that genuinely hands over control of the projects to the people who will benefit by them. In this way the agencies are releasing their hold on power. They are diminishing their grasp on the sources of domination in order that others may grow as people. This, too, is a graphic example of the end of aggression in relationships between communities.

Many more examples could be given, if one had more space. The struggle for a more just and harmonious society in the future depends on being able to overcome the ingrained tendency of human beings to panic in the face of threats to their sense of security. Such a change can happen only when increasing numbers of ordinary people in the Western world open themselves to the new kind of order that Jesus Christ gave his life to create.

We turn next to look in some detail at the shape of this new order and how it applies to the kind of world we have been describing.

3: Why the tide has turned

A rediscovery of the kingdom of God

Everywhere one turns in the Church today the theme of the kingdom of God is being discussed. The idea of a kingdom and a monarch may not fit well with people's longings for more democratic societies; nevertheless, the reality that lies behind the language of kingdom and king in the Bible is again capturing the imagination of Christians.

In 1980 the World Council of Churches hosted a mission conference in Melbourne whose theme was 'Your Kingdom Come'. As long ago as 1972 the Latin American Theological Fraternity, an evangelical body, organised a consultation in Lima on the subject of the kingdom of God and Latin America today. Anglo-Catholics in the Jubilee Fellowship in Britain, following the Christian socialist tradition of people like Conrad Noel, emphasise the centrality of the kingdom in their theological and political thinking.

A rediscovery of the kingdom of God by widely different groups within the churches does not mean that everyone is agreed about its meaning and significance. Christians of all persuasions have a tendency to stress whatever fits most easily into their particular concerns and activities. The kingdom, like other biblical ideas, can be interpreted to mean rather different things. There are those, particularly some evangelical Christians, who hardly stress the kingdom at all, because it does not seem to play a very central part in the New Testament writings outside of the first three Gospels.

Reasons for the comparative absence of the theme of the kingdom in the letters of the New Testament will occupy us in the next chapter. First, however, we will try to discover why the kingdom is becoming once again a prominent part of the way the Church understands itself and its task.

The experience of Third World Christians

First, the growing participation of Third World Christian leaders in the councils of world-wide Church bodies has brought to the fore the political and social implications of the gospel. Christians in the Third World have been unavoidably caught up in the political turmoil which, since the Second World War, has catapulted many of their countries into full independence. Identification with the hopes and struggles of their own people has given Christians in various parts of the world a new agenda for their theological reflection. Also, the debate begun seriously in the 1960s about the causes of acute deprivation in underdeveloped nations has been centred on the exercise of political and economic power.

In this over-all context Christ's preaching of the kingdom – God's new age of justice, peace and partnership – has seemed to be the most relevant key for discovering how Christians should respond to volatile political situations.

Belief in political solutions

Secondly, the Western world in the last two decades has witnessed a notable 'politicisation' of life. As other values get crowded out, or eroded away, the power of political decision to remake the world has become increasingly attractive. Politicians, legislators and the bureaucratic institutions of the state are either invested with the sole responsibility of producing genuine change and of solving all manner of problems, or else they are condemned as the main obstacles in the way of a fairer and more prosperous society. The gods who determine the fate of humans have become mortals. However, though often vilified and debunked, they are still expected to possess god-like qualities. Those in opposition (whether a political party in a parliamentary democracy or guerrillas fighting a dictatorship) are confident of being able to solve most of the pressing problems of the nation – at least as long as they remain in opposition.

Political intervention in normal market economic procedures, particularly since the first large rise in oil prices in 1973, has become increasingly necessary. Western governments, even when their political philosophy indicates a course of non-interference, have to promote policies whose intention is to reverse the particularly deep and catastrophic consequences of recession for advanced industrial nations. They are no longer able to maintain a kind of neutral stance, holding the ring, while industry plans and initiates sustained, long-term growth.

This increased expectation that political life holds the key to the future of human communities results in short-term political strategies replacing stable long-term political goals. In a situation where clear ethical guidelines for the use of power are lacking those directly involved in political affairs will tend to concentrate on matters of most immediate concern.

These are inevitably defined in relationship to the freedom to consume that society has tacitly agreed is the chief value to be conserved. To remain high in the popular ratings politicians have almost no option but to defend everyone's standard of living against the loss of real earnings.

Present economic strategies, however different they may appear (whether monetarist, protectionist or reflationary), are only distinct means to the same end. The end itself is rarely debated, except perhaps by rather fringe groups like the anti-nuclear lobby and ecology parties. I believe this is mainly due to the fact that a pleasure-seeking lifestyle has influenced our opinions for so long that we have lost our memory for an ethic which exalts values like generosity, self-sacrifice, restraint, equality, solidarity and personal creativity. There is a sense in which political debate and decision-making in a democratic society does little more than reflect majority opinion about life's meaning and an acceptable code of moral behaviour. Such an opinion can be expressed not only positively but also by default, by people refusing to challenge the policies of the moment.

Christians in the West have been forced by the effects of both today's economic crisis and ethical confusion to become involved in political discussion and action. Searching for guidelines to direct their thinking on matters formerly taken up by a few enthusiasts who felt a vocation for politics, Christians have discovered that a deep-seated tendency to divorce faith from public life has left them naked in the public arena of political debate.

Biblical doctrines like justification and regeneration, fundamental though they are for understanding the meaning of personal salvation, are not alone sufficient to give clear principles for social action in a political scene characterised by power struggles, pragmatism, personal ambition and secular ideologies. The concept of the kingdom, however its relevance may be understood in detail, gives a solid point of reference for debating both long-term and short-

term social and political issues. We will seek to verify this claim
when we look at the meaning of the kingdom in the next chapter.

Structures are not neutral: the challenge of Marxism

Thirdly, in the last twenty years a sizeable shift in emphasis has
taken place in Christian teaching and preaching from concern about
individual salvation and personal integrity to concern about the
dehumanising effects of structures.

The greatest single catalyst producing this change has been a new
'humanist' Marxism. Once Christians ceased to identify everything
Marx taught with everything communist regimes practise, they
became open to hearing a Marxist criticism of society. Once they
realised that a good deal of Marx's analysis of economic reality is
not dependent upon his atheistic views they began to appreciate
that what he said in areas other than philosophy could be correct.
As Dom Helder Camara (1982) has put it, 'when someone . . .
irresistibly attracts millions of human beings, when he inspires the
life and death of a great part of mankind, and makes the powerful
of the earth tremble with hate and fear, that man deserves to be
studied'.

The challenge of Marxism to Christian thought comes principally
in four ways. First, it presents itself as a strong defender of the
dignity of human beings. Every person has a right to develop himself
freely and enjoy the fruit of his work. The present capitalist system
is incompatible with these goals, because working people are used
as mere instruments to produce wealth for another's pleasure. The
worker, because he does not own what he produces, is alienated
from himself as a person who creates. He is also fundamentally at
odds with his fellow human beings because his interests conflict
with those of another class. The only way in which people's deep-
seated personal and social alienation can be overcome is by replacing the capitalist system of economic life with a socialist one.

Marxism appears to be an ideology with a deep compassion for
people. Unlike present political systems – big business, even the
Church – it does not seem to have any particular vested interests
to defend. It poses itself as the only true force for reconciling man
with himself and with others. Marxism challenges Christians to
understand and deal with the social dimension of man's lostness.
The restoration of human wholeness to which the biblical message
of salvation points cannot be achieved without an adequate response

to the breakdown of community relationships. This breakdown is due to social and economic factors and not just personal ones.

Secondly, it is uncompromising in its analysis of the causes and cure of inequality and oppression among humans. The real reason for their existence is not outmoded religious beliefs, political structures or social customs, but economic relations. Permanent change to a just and compassionate sharing of wealth is dependent upon knowing what is the fundamental problem. Marxism claims to be a strictly scientific analysis of the way in which economic systems work either to engender or to end inequality, dependence and conflict.

Thirdly, it contains a strong element of hope. Marxist analysis claims to demonstrate that change towards a reconciled humanity is written into the way production is organised. Marxists believe the goal of history is assured. A new world order is inevitable. Then the producers of wealth will finally become also the owners. In that day, they maintain, classes as we now know them will disappear. The basic antagonisms of society will cease. Marxism's crowning assertion is that Communist society is the only place where man can find his own real humanity by discovering that of his neighbour.

Fourthly, it is openly hostile to the practice of religion and to belief in God. Marx once said that 'the criticism of religion is the premise of all criticism'. He was concerned with the kind of religion on offer in his native Germany: a religion firmly in the hands of those who controlled the movement of wealth to their own advantage. Marxists believe that religion must always play the role of defending society as it is, and thus of backing a system of exploitation. Of necessity, religion is 'opium for the people'. It provides an interpretation of the world which allows both the rich to justify their style of life and the poor to grasp hold of a substitute which helps them accept and endure their plight.

Moreover, Marxists are usually militant atheists (though socialism bears no logical nor historical relationship to atheism). They believe man is alone in the universe. There is no other sphere of reality but this world. Man is answerable only to himself. There is no ethic higher than that which man creates to regulate his own life. Marx once said, 'man is the highest being to man'. Marxists interpret all talk about God as a projection of man's feeling of weakness and dependence in a world he does not understand and cannot control. God is man's attempt to compensate for his feelings of alienation on earth, until he understands that it has a purely social explanation.

These four main challenges are powerful. Some people brought up as Christians have decided that Marxism is a more coherent and relevant way of looking at the meaning of life than is the faith they inherited. A colleague of mine in Argentina once gave a lecture on Christian faith and Marxism to a group of university students. He discovered afterwards that three out of the five leading Marxists among the students came from Christian homes. They had found Marxism to be a more realistic response to basic human needs than the message they heard at home and in church.

Of course, from a Christian point of view, the Marxist analysis of human relations misses the fundamental cause of alienation. Marxism concentrates too exclusively on economic factors. It leaves out of account the fact that human beings exploit one another, not because a particular economic order allows them to, but because the desire is deeply rooted in their nature. The particular means of production which exploits has been created by human beings. It is not the result of impersonal historical forces. As has been wittily observed, in Capitalism man exploits man; in Communism it is the other way around!

Marxists, therefore, confuse the occasion for exploitation with its cause. They eloquently describe *how* it happens, but give no adequate reason *why* some see it in their best interests to abuse the rights and dignity of others.

Human beings, failing to acknowledge the Creator, deny their status as creatures, on an equal footing with every other person. Denying they are accountable to God, they believe they can accumulate power to themselves and, thus, dictate the destiny of others.

Communism, therefore, as empirical observation affirms, can never lead to human emancipation from a false world. It simply provides different opportunities for exploitation and the manifestation of a bourgeois spirit.

The scope of the kingdom of God

In a world in which to feed the hungry, clothe the naked, house the homeless, heal the sick and help the uneducated to learn is of primary concern, a message confined to individual reconciliation with God and hope of a reversal of fortune in another life has shown itself to be totally inadequate. So Christians have begun to ask the question, 'Is there life before death'? How can it be achieved? What are the conditions?

From within a world of misery, hopelessness and helplessness some Christians began to look afresh at the whole Bible. There to their surprise and delight they discovered themes like justice, oppression and liberation, which they thought had been invented by political extremists. They began to wonder whether Marxists had not stolen their clothes.

The question then became how one was able to fit together all that the Bible says about social issues with its equally clear emphasis on the need for each individual to change his selfish way of life and receive from God forgiveness for wrong-doing and a new spirit.

The answer that the Bible gives is the reality of the kingdom. The kingdom sums up God's plan to create a new human life by making possible a new kind of community among people, families and groups. The theme of the kingdom brings together a number of crucial concerns: the possibility of a personal relationship to Jesus; with man's responsibility to manage wisely the whole of nature; the expectation that real change is possible here and now; a realistic assessment of the strength of opposition to God's intentions; the creation of new human relationships and the eventual liberation by God of the whole of nature from corruption.

In a remarkable way the kingdom seems to provide a unique framework into which one may fit both biblical and modern concerns. It also deals with the issues raised by Marxist social analysis and shows why it is not radical enough. In the next chapter we will argue the case that the kingdom is central to the message of the gospel, and show why many Christians are convinced that it is the only complete answer to mankind's search for an end to alienation, violence and corruption.

4: Exploring the interior

There is no doubt that we now come to the heart of the matter. So far we have tried to set the scene by looking at some of the major characteristics of the world today and reasons why Christians are rediscovering the theme of God's kingdom.

To show the essential place of the kingdom both in understanding the way the world works and in regulating the Church's task we need to survey carefully the biblical material. (I realise, of course, that at the moment discussion about the meaning and implications of the kingdom is controversial. We will try to meet this fact as we go along.) The intention of this chapter is to demonstrate that the meaning of Christian faith is wholly dependent upon grasping and applying the reality of the kingdom to contemporary life. That is a big claim. We will try to produce the evidence to justify it.

The obvious place to begin is with the generally agreed fact that Jesus saw all that he did and said in the light of God's kingdom.

Jesus did not so much define the kingdom as announce its coming: 'the Kingdom of God is near' (Mark 1.15); 'I must preach the Good News of the Kingdom of God . . . because that is what God sent me to do' (Luke 4.43). There is no detailed explanation to be found at any point in his teaching. On the other hand, his whole life was full of clues about the kingdom. When pieced together they give a fairly complete picture of what he meant. Were this not so, his life would be a complete enigma.

The kingdom is not an idea Jesus invented. He assumes the long-standing expectation of his own people that God would establish his rule on earth. How one understands Jesus' preaching of the kingdom depends in the first place on how one understands what the Jewish Scriptures say about it. This was clearly the basis from which Jesus himself worked.

Jesus both filled out the meaning of the original promises of the Old Testament and also consciously fulfilled them (Matt. 5.17). Many people go astray in their interpretation of the kingdom because they do not give sufficient weight to the fact that Jesus accepted the teaching of the Old Testament and built upon it. For example, over many generations Christians have been fed on the notion that the kingdom refers primarily to an individual experience of God's rule over their lives and secondarily to a heaven of peace and reconciliation at the end of time. Attention to the Old Testament would have given them a much more complete picture. From there they would have learnt that the kingdom is all about a new created order that touches every aspect of life, applicable in the present as well as in the future. An inadequate grasp of the kingdom is, then, the direct result of ignorance of the Scriptures. The consequences for the life and work of the Church have been disastrous.

God's rule in the history of the Jewish people

The kingdom in the Old Testament is associated with God's rule over the universe, over the nations and over Israel. God's control of nature is total (Ps. 103.19). He orders and controls the life of every nation (Amos 1–2; Isa. 19.24–5). He intervenes and plans the well-being of his specially chosen people. God's rule is hindered, but not finally thwarted, by the fact that human creation has rebelled against him.

The first specific mention of God's kingly rule comes in the song of Moses and the people after the crossing of the Sea (Exod. 15.8). It is confirmed in the famous terms of the covenant: 'you shall be my own possession among all peoples; for all the earth is mine, and you shall be to me a kingdom of priests and a holy nation' (Exod. 19.5–6; RSV).

God's kingship over everything created is closely linked to the events of the Exodus and the covenant. Later on when the Hebrew people demanded their own king (to be like everyone else) God reminds them that they have rejected him as king, the one known especially by the fact that he 'rescued you from the Egyptians and all the other peoples who were oppressing you' (1 Sam. 10.17–19; 8.4–9).

Throughout the Old Testament God's kingship is seen in close relationship to the exercise of authority and power by human kings. Sometimes this was seen as beneficial, as in the case of David and a handful of others (2 Sam. 7.4–7; 2 Kgs. 18.3ff; 22.2), but mostly their reigns were characterised by an abandonment of God's rule of justice (2 Kgs. 16.1–4).

Samuel predicted that the experiment of monarchy in Israel would be ruinous (1 Sam. 8.11–18). What he said tragically came true. Successive kings treated God's people just as the Pharaohs of Egypt had done. They trampled on the terms of the covenant, they forced the people into slavery again, they mocked God.

Much of what is recorded about God in the Old Testament is in contrast to the people's daily experience of human authority and power. This fact is vitally important, for often God's kingly rule is portrayed by modern commentators in too vague a way. Even when it is seen in terms of God's demand for general moral values, like the ending of greed, envy, pride, lust and hate, it is hazy and out of focus. In contrast, God's reign has to do with the specific way a society should operate. The Old Testament is a record of concrete events interpreted by people specially chosen by God to communicate their meaning. God's kingdom is manifest in these events. It cannot, therefore, be defined abstractly as 'where God reigns'. It is rather 'the particular way God's reign takes shape in different circumstances'.

Psalms 145 and 146 provide a good example. They remind us that the essence of God's power is to satisfy people's basic needs, to uphold justice and equity, to judge in favour of the oppressed, to give food to the hungry, to set prisoners free, to protect strangers and to help widows and orphans. This is the concrete reality of God's 'everlasting kingdom' and his 'rule which is for ever' (Ps. 145.12–13).

The kings abandoned precisely these tasks. Again and again they were rebuked and challenged to face their responsibilities: 'stop doing evil and learn to do right. See that justice is done – help those who are oppressed, give orphans their rights, and defend widows' (Isa. 1.17).

God's rule has to do with daily political and social events. Everyone should be guaranteed the possibility of enjoying part of God's creation – 'among his own vineyards and fig-trees' (Mic. 4.4). Industries devoted to manufacturing weapons of destruction should develop technology to aid human development (Mic. 4.3). The law and legal processes should not be weighted in favour of the wealthy (Mic. 6.9–7.3). Teachers should remind their pupils that the true source of wisdom lies in acknowledging God, and that justice exalts a nation.

God's kingdom is the detailed expression of his caring oversight of all life. Because rulers did not recognise their responsibility to pursue a policy of equality and welfare among their people, but used their position to amass wealth for themselves (Isa. 5.8; Mic. 2.2), God got rid of them. In their place he has appointed another ruler who will 'see that justice is done on earth' (Isa. 42.1–7).

This king shares God's nature exactly and will carry through his plans perfectly – 'a child is born to us . . . and he will be our ruler. . . . His royal power will continue to grow; his kingdom will always be at peace. He will rule as King David's successor basing his power on right and justice' (Isa. 9.6–7).

God's special representative (the Messiah) is spoken of many times in the Psalms and the Prophets. His principal task is to proclaim and bring to pass God's time of salvation (Isa. 61.2). This time will be marked both by judgment and a new creation (Zech. 9.9–17). There will be universal peace and prosperity, embracing man's relationship to God, to nature (Isa. 11.6–9) and to fellow human beings. God's covenant with his people and with creation will then finally be fulfilled (Mal. 3.1).

Naturally, the vision of the kingdom painted in many Old Testament passages belongs to a future period. The kingdom will be the consummation of world history when the earth will be transformed. The kingdom, however, is not postponed. Its reality, as we have seen, is already present in God's just and compassionate ordering of daily life. It is the effective execution of his love. It is the reversal of all the consequences of evil: death, disease, plagues, famine, enmity, exploitation, idolatry, sexual deviations, violence, culpable ignorance, lies, prejudice, self-righteousness and empty religious practices. It is the establishing of a new kind of community based on open and generous sharing in line with such legislation as that for the sabbatical and jubilee years (Lev. 25; Deut. 15). Supremely, in the experience of the Jewish people, it contrasts totally with the life they suffered in Egypt. It is the wholeness of created life as God has always intended it.

Jesus and his contemporaries clash over the meaning of the kingdom

So when Jesus began to announce that 'the kingdom of God is upon you', 'for the time has now come' (NEB), he aroused enormous expectations. Can this be the Messiah?

John, in particular, records in his Gospel how public opinion was divided over the significance of Jesus of Nazareth. To many, Jesus appeared to interpret his vocation as Messiah to inaugurate the kingdom in an unacceptable manner.

The salvation of the new age was increasingly being interpreted by his kinsfolk in nationalistic terms because of the odious occupation of the promised land (after 63 BC) by the heathen force of Rome. As under the Maccabees, 150 years earlier, many Jews believed God would drive out their enemies, restore Israel's fortunes and give them security to observe the Law.

Judas, the Galilean, one of those who led a revolt against Roman rule, believed that God's kingdom meant that no one other than God should be obeyed. This led him to justify using violence to free the people from the yoke of an alien power.

The nationalistic version of the kingdom can be described as a backward-looking Utopia. It intended a return to the splendours of David and Solomon's reigns. The ideal was a nation under God cut off from the wicked ways of the rest of the world. This dream was perhaps still with Jesus' disciples when they asked the question, 'Lord, will you at this time give the Kingdom back to Israel?' (Acts 1.6). They had recognised Jesus to be the Messiah. They knew that the Messiah would establish the kingdom. However, they had not yet seen the kingdom as they expected it: the righteous vindicated, the wicked destroyed and the nations coming to Jerusalem to learn the Law.

Jesus' ministry took place against a background of intense nationalism. He was aware of the danger that the God of the universe could be converted into nothing more than a local tribal deity. Hence he had to begin by correcting a mistaken view of God's reign.

He emphasised, first, that the kingdom is meant for all people. At the heart of the conflict over Jesus was his scandalous view that God's love and plan of salvation extended to every human being whatever they did. Such a view nearly led to his death at the beginning of his public life. One sabbath in the synagogue in Nazareth (Luke 4.18–30) Jesus read the Scriptures out loud. The passage was from Isaiah 61. At first what he said seemed to be accepted. Later, however, he met fierce opposition and total rejection. In most versions of what happened it is difficult to see why his listeners should have changed their attitude so quickly. Someone has suggested, therefore, that the actual reaction of the people was that 'all were especially struck by what he said, and were astonished that he spoke about grace'.

Had Jesus completed the quotation from Isaiah he would have announced 'vengeance on Israel's enemies'. Understanding the kingdom in this way was at the heart of Jewish nationalistic sentiments. However, as Jesus went on to state, the examples of God's dealings with the widow of Sarepta and Naaman, the Syrian, demonstrate that the Messianic age announced by Isaiah overflows the bounds of Israel. The kingdom is all about a new, universal community. God's relationship to all people is one based on grace, not on merit or vengeance. The truth of Jesus' message cannot be measured by the narrow standards of current Jewish thinking. Jon Sobrino powerfully states the alternatives in this way:

> Jesus shared the conviction of the Zealots that God's kingdom had to be established . . . but his conception of God was very different from theirs. . . . Rather then advocating the complete abolition of the Zealot spirit, he proposes an alternative to Zealotism. . . . He was interested in something more than retributive justice. He wanted renewal and recreation.
>
> In Jesus' eyes God's ultimate historical word is love, whereas the ultimate historical word of power in the human world is oppression. (1978: 369–70)

And, we might add, this is true however good the intention may be.

Secondly, on one memorable occasion, Jesus stated that his 'kingdom is not of this world' (John 18.36). This saying has often been completely misunderstood. Many people have interpreted it to mean that the kingdom has nothing to do with present society. They believe that Jesus was talking about either an inner, spiritual reality, a person's individual right relationship to God – as if he had said 'the kingdom is *within* you' rather than '*among* you' (Luke 17.21) – or the reality of another existence, beyond history. This text in John's Gospel has been made into the major piece of evidence that Jesus never intended his mission to bear directly on the kinds of political and economic decisions that affect everyday life.

This, however, is the very opposite of what Jesus was contending for. He stood before Pontius Pilate, the local representative of the Emperor's universal authority. There he joined issue with Pilate over the meaning of truth and falsehood, particularly in relationship to what constitutes power. The 'world' (a common expression in John's Gospel) believes that power is vested in three things: the capacity to make and enforce law (John 7.49); the superiority of one race over another (John 8.33), and the ability to subject others to your will by physical force (John 19.10–11).

So, when Jesus told Pilate, 'my kingdom is not of this world', he declared very simply that his kingdom is not based on this fundamental lie about what constitutes power and freedom. The kingdom cannot be established by power as the world wields it. Its power does not spring from (of) this world.

The kingdom of Jesus, therefore, offers an alternative way of life and different values to those of the kingdom of this world; not, however, as a spiritual existence removed from real life, nor as a remote reality of some distant future, but as an alternative society organised socially according to the way of Jesus. Not only Pilate, but also the Jews, had to learn how God meant the human community to operate under his rule.

Some people have questioned whether Jesus really saw himself as the Messiah come to inaugurate God's new age. A Jewish scholar, Flusser (1969: 87), has no such hesitation. He says: 'Jesus is the only Jew who is known from ancient times to have proclaimed that the new age of salvation had already begun.'

Serious doubts about the reporting of the Gospels could only be entertained if one was prepared to exclude systematically all the evidence that Jesus displayed a new, unique power in his relationship to people, events and nature. To dismiss this evidence would show an arbitrary and wilful disregard for careful historical investigation. Everything he said and did was directly related to the coming of the kingdom. He reversed all the consequences of evil in the world: disease, possession by inhuman spirits, guilt, ritualistic and empty religion, a caste system of purity and impurity, scarcity of food, a hostile nature, commercial exploitation and death.

In these activities Jesus showed that he believed that the goal of God's kingly rule is the complete remaking of the universe. Mark, in particular, sees Jesus as the second Adam. Leaving behind the desert and a struggle with wild animals (both express the opposite of the original creation with its fertile garden and tame creatures), and beginning with the defeat of the tempter (Mark 1.12–13), Jesus reverses all the effects of the first Adam's disobedience.

In Jesus the powers of the new age are already at work in the world. Perhaps the most explicit evidence of the kingdom is the hostility it arouses from those who feel secure in the age of sin and death (Matt. 11.12; John 15.18–21; 16.1–4). The new age threatens everything they own and trust in. Those who belong to this world are those who have shared out its riches and privileges among themselves: the wealthy, political rulers, religious leaders, the wise and understanding (Mark 10.21–3; Matt. 6.5; Matt. 11.25–6; 23.5–7; Luke 16.25; 18.11–12). To enter the kingdom they must become like children – that is, as those who possess nothing. As they have so much to give up – wealth, power, prestige, privilege and knowledge – they will find it virtually impossible to leave the foremost positions in one age to become 'the least in the kingdom' (Mark 10.21–3; Matt. 11.11).

As long as a person treasures that which is on earth – riches, family, religious practices, wisdom, political power or his own life it is impossible to inherit the kingdom. . . . A person cannot abandon what he loves most. . . . That is why entrance into the kingdom is impossible (on one's own). . . . God alone can so free people that they fulfil the conditions (for entry). . . . The power of God to transform and enable is itself a blessing of the kingdom. (Piper, 1979: 76ff)

To sum up, we can say that whenever the kingdom is present the values and structures which are characteristic of the present age will be reversed (Luke 1.51–3). Alternatively, wherever these are being challenged and turned round there is a sign of the presence of the kingdom.

The prominence of the kingdom in the life and preaching of Jesus was extended both to his closest disciples (Luke 9.2) and to a wider group (Luke 10.9–11). It was part of the message of the first Christians following Jesus' resurrection, though mentioned less often (Acts 1.3; 8.12; 14.22; 19.8; 20.25; 28.23, 31). It is significant, however, that Luke opens and closes his account of the way the witness of the first Christians to Jesus expanded with reference to the kingdom. We may take it that he saw this as the core of the message of the early Church.

Reasons why Paul refers only occasionally to the kingdom

A problem, however, arises in the case of Paul. In comparison with other themes he mentions the kingdom by name only a few times (fourteen in all). If the entire message of Scripture can be rightly understood only in terms of God's kingdom, as we are claiming, this apparent absence needs some explaining.

Naturally, no one can be certain why Paul used the word so infrequently. Three possibilities come to mind. First, Paul may have simply taken Jesus' teaching about the kingdom for granted. He cannot have been unaware of it. There is certainly nothing particularly surprising about the story of Paul in Rome explaining to local Jewish leaders the message about the Kingdom of God, and . . . about Jesus' (Acts 28.23).

When he shared the Gospel he had been proclaiming with the Church in Rome one may assume that he was talking about the 'good news of the kingdom'. Where he does mention the kingdom in this letter (Rom. 14.17) he seems to base his discussion on Jesus' teaching in the Sermon on the Mount (Matt. 5.6, 9, 10, 12; 6.31 with 5.20 and 6.33). The whole passage (Rom. 14.1ff) is in part an exposition of Jesus saying: 'There is nothing that goes into a person from the outside which can make him ritually unclean' (Mark 7.15). Paul is convinced that the coming of the kingdom has cancelled out a world concerned about regulating in minute detail eating and drinking habits. It spells freedom from this kind of preoccupation, because Jesus was the very embodiment of this freedom in his own life.

In another letter Paul recognises the importance of Psalm 110 as announcing the kingdom. Here the kingdom marks the defeat of all God's enemies, of which death is the last classic example (1 Cor. 15.24–8). As Paul in this passage unfolds his major teaching on the Resurrection, he probably sees Jesus' triumph over death as the moment when the Messiah is finally crowned king of the new age. In quoting from Psalm 110 and alluding to other Psalms that speak of the coronation of the king, Paul acknowledges the same Old Testament passages as those used by Jesus. We may, perhaps, guess that the Christians to whom he was writing needed no further specific mention of the kingdom than the few times it occurs.

Secondly, it is likely, although admittedly this is an argument from silence, that Paul did not want to use the term kingdom for largely Gentile congregations. Such an idea, after all, would not have made as much sense in the political context of Greek city-states as in that of Jewish history. There is plenty of evidence in Paul's letters that he was careful to use language that was already current amongst Christian converts. Where Paul does actually use the word kingdom it is usually to summarise an argument and punch it home.

Thirdly, and this is the most important aspect, Paul, who was clearly an original thinker, used different terminology to convey exactly the same reality as that expressed by the kingdom. Everything that Paul says fits naturally into the major consideration that in the life, death and resurrection of Jesus, the Messiah, the kingdom has arrived. If one had space one could easily demonstrate that such central ideas in Paul's teaching as the relationship between Adam and Christ (the two ages), the redemption of creation (Rom. 8.18ff), the victory of Christ over the powers (Rom. 8.38ff; Col. 2.15), and the life of the new community (Gal. 3.28; Eph. 2.13–18; Col. 3.10–11) are natural extensions of what we can discover else-where about the kingdom. Indeed, I would be bold enough to claim that Paul's understanding of the meaning of Jesus Christ can only be grasped against the background of the reality of the kingdom.

If these suggestions are accepted, then our claim that Jesus' inauguration of the kingdom is the central message of the early Church is not challenged by the relative absence of one word in Paul's letters. We need to remind ourselves that a Jew from an orthodox background, like Paul, could not have accepted that Jesus was the Messiah without accepting that the kingdom had come with him. No kingdom, no Messiah! What convinced Paul that Jesus was the Messiah was the Resurrection. He was forced to admit that the reality of the age to come was already in evidence around him. So, he wrote, 'upon us the fulfilment of the ages has come' (1 Cor. 10.11; NEB).

The challenge of the kingdom to the Church

The importance of understanding what the biblical writers mean when they talk about the kingdom cannot be overstated. It should revolutionise the Church's attitude to and strategy towards what it thinks it is about. For too long Christians of most traditions have accepted and communicated a deficient message. Neither theologically, nor practically, do they seem to have been able to make much sense of the relationship between social and personal salvation, between spiritual life and the material world, between God's action in the present and in the future, between evangelism as the communication of words and as compassionate caring for the physical welfare of people.

The results have been quite disastrous. Different sections of the Church do what they think is the most important task, while others accuse them of betraying the gospel. Some Christians establish a list of priorities for the Church as if by paying attention to the top of the chart one could justify the neglect of items further down. The Lausanne Covenant, for example, asserts that 'in the church's mission of sacrificial service evangelism is primary'. I will argue later that this attempt to give priority to one aspect of the Church's mission arises from too narrow an understanding of evangelism. This is at the root of the contemporary Church's failure to bring together the activities of making disciples and of changing society in the direction of God's will.

The way the Church continues to pose alternatives shows it is still working with the wrong kind of theoretical framework. It looks at reality basically as if it were two tiers of a cake, one on top of the other. The bottom tier is the material world – corrupt, the source of temptation, destined to disappear. The top tier is the spiritual world – pure, the place of God's existence, the destination of all who truly believe. The Christian ideal, according to this model, becomes an escape from material human existence here and now to a spiritual realm whose complete reality is future. Those who hold this view are convinced that the believer is on a journey from earth to heaven.

This, or anything like it, is not, I submit, how the Bible looks at reality. For the Bible the place of God's activity is the material world. Human beings are, for all time, physical beings. This world has been taken over and distorted by powers hostile to the goodness and justice of God. They belong, however, to an order of life that is passing away, condemned by God. Another kind of order is already active in God's creation. One day it will have full sway. When that happens, earth will not have become heaven, but heaven will have become the earth! Believers will not journey one by one to God in another place, but God will come to be more and more fully with his people. This I take to be the meaning behind the vision of Revelation 21.1–5.

In Parts Three and Four we will explore the implications of this change of view about the way one conceives the relationship between God and his world for the Church's responsibility towards the world of which it is a part.

5: Luxury apartments and desolate slums

In Lima they call them 'young colonies', in Buenos Aires 'wretched towns'. Around every major city in the majority of nations they sprawl in every direction. They are the growing shanty towns caused by the rapid influx of people from rural areas.

The mile upon mile of precarious housing is most obviously characterised by what it lacks. There are no proper streets, only dirt tracks. After a tropical storm these become an impassable quagmire of mud, small lakes and torrential streams. There may be intermittent lighting where some enterprising families have pirated a source direct from the national system. No permanent electricity is, however, available. There is no water piped to people's living accommodation. There may be a communal tap somewhere down one of the tracks. It is reported that in some places it is easier to get hold of Coca Cola than drinking water. There is no drainage system. The dwelling places of the people cannot be called houses in the recognised sense of the word. The floors are mud; the walls are made of cardboard, or some other flimsy material; the roofs are makeshift and far from waterproof. Here you may find as many as twenty adults and children living in two rooms.

Visiting these huge settlements and being entertained in some of the precarious dwellings brings home directly the appalling scandal of a society that allows a high proportion of its inhabitants to live in conditions that stunt physical growth, encourage disease and often bring early death.

The desolate slums are a blight for another reason as well. Close beside them in some cities, far removed in others, are magnificent mansions and luxury apartments. Along the spacious avenue, Libertador, in the suburb of Palermo in Buenos Aires are four-, five- and six-bedroomed flats. The latest in household luxuries are installed, including in some cases sauna baths. They look out over the park to the river beyond. Transport facilities in and out of town are good. Most families have a living-in maid. For good measure they may well own a holiday home in the delta area outside Buenos Aires known as the Tigre, or another flat in the seaside resort of Mar del Plata or Villa Gessel, or a farm somewhere in the vast pampa region.

Reasons for justifying inequalities

The real scandal of the poor in the world today is not only their poverty and the misery it creates, but the ostentatious affluence of the rich. Our moral credulity is stretched to breaking-point by those who want to find reasons for justifying the incredible difference in lifestyle existing between the poor majority and the rich minority of almost every nation.

The well-to-do have generally adopted one of two attitudes towards the situation. Many people in the Western world, being cushioned against seeing vast extremes of wealth, imagine that the situation is not as bad as usually portrayed. They manage to persuade themselves that the conditions and figures quoted are either exaggerated or distorted for reasons of political propaganda. They also look for crumbs of comfort, such as the resettlement of shanty-town dwellers in more solid accommodation (though often this is done forcibly without consultation), or the setting up of government clinics for a mass immunisation campaign. The point, however, of these well advertised events is precisely that they are crumbs. At best, they are rare acts of charity; at worst, attempts to remove causes of acute embarrassment to governments.

The privileged class of the Third World, who cannot avert their eyes from what lies just beyond their doorstep, develop a siege mentality. This takes both a literal and metaphorical form. Many of them live in houses surrounded by high walls covered by broken glass. Entrance to the grounds is by an electrically operated iron gate. At night Alsatian dogs roam the garden. Sometimes armed guards are on duty in the street outside.

More significant, perhaps, are the mental defence-mechanisms that are set in motion whenever anyone challenges the huge discrepancies between the standard of life they enjoy and the lot of most of their compatriots. They desperately cling on to any argument that will justify their keeping what they own. These arguments may vary, but usually they can be summarised in four main statements.

First, the wealth a person owns is due to a long period of exacting study and subsequent hard work. The implication of this argument is that affluence is directly related to a person's willingness to expend time and energy in the pursuit of accumulating purchasing power. Poverty, on the other hand, is the consequence of a person's conscious decision to work a minimal amount of time to keep body and soul together. The assumption is that, if they cared to, everyone has a chance to 'make good' in life. All that is needed is ambition, resilience and perseverance. These are traits potentially open to everyone.

Secondly, following on from the preceding argument, the right to own what one has acquired by hard work is defended as the most basic right of a 'free' society. Attempts to suggest that there should be limits to any one person's or family's level of possessions are savagely attacked as an interference in the right of private property.

Thirdly, the spectre of international communism soon appears on the horizon. Discussion of a more equal society is dismissed as the desire to install a regime that not only restricts the free flow of capital, but hedges about every other freedom as well. Those who would opt for an economic order in which wealth is more evenly distributed across all sections of society (a fairly obvious and not desperately radical moral imperative) are then made to defend themselves against accusations of being dangerous subversives whose aim is to overthrow an order based on absolute moral values. If the consequences that flow from the charge (slander in the press, abduction, torture, imprisonment without trial, loss of citizenship, exile or death) were not so serious, the accusation itself would be laughable. In point of fact, it is the existing order of gross inequality that displays a ruthless pragmatism and disdain of moral standards.

Fourthly, and as a last resort, some would argue that those who possess the resources for creating wealth are the ones who have proved themselves capable of using them wisely. They give themselves credit for an innate genius in the investment of finance, the creation of work for others and the development of a modern infrastructure that will benefit all. The rest neither could, nor would they care to, exercise this enormous responsibility. They have demonstrated their inability to handle property and wealth by the ease with which they squander what little they have owned.

So much for the arguments. Together they make up a classic example of how ideology works. Ideology is an attempt to defend rationally the vested interests of a group who control power in society. It acts like a guard-dog trained to spring at the throat of an intruder. Its natural environment is violence, for it is more concerned about retaining a hold on power by any means, than about promoting truth. Repressive regimes in the Third World are not acting in defence of a genuinely free society against the threat of totalitarian forces, but to ensure that what has been gained by the sector whose interest they defend is not snatched away. Like cornered animals the viciousness of the attack is in proportion to the falseness of the situation they seek to defend.

The real causes of poverty

The horrific statistics describing the plight of the poor have been published so often that it is unnecessary to repeat the figures here. Even allowing for the difficulty of collecting accurate data and for the possibility of exaggeration, the gulf between members of the same human race remains vast, and is increasing. The facts are important. It is, however, more vital to discover the causes and look for likely cures.

The standard explanation given by economists in the neo-classical tradition of capitalism for the existence of poverty in a world also experiencing abundance is that productive capacity in some areas has not yet been developed to its full potential. This may be due to lack of technological expertise, inadequate access to reasonably priced natural resources or to a culture that does not reward hard work. Poverty can only be ended, so the argument goes, when there is a marked rise in the creation of wealth.

The assumption on which the analysis is based is that poverty should be defined as scarcity, what some people lack. A parallel is then drawn between the way one country has developed (say Britain or Japan) and what is possible in another. Supplying what is lacking – capital accumulation, technology, basic infrastructures – is only a matter of time and good management. What the poor countries need is a helping hand to struggle on upwards to the crest of the hill and the plateau beyond.

Socialist economists, on the other hand, give different reasons for the persistence of underdevelopment. Fundamental to their analysis of the way modern economic systems work is a theory of conflict. Whereas capitalist economics, based on a belief in natural market forces, maintains that what is good for some is good for all, socialism points to the considerable historical evidence which shows that one cannot maximise one's own advantage without causing deprivation and suffering to another.

The fundamental belief of capitalist economics is that the basic economic problem is the way scarce resources are allocated among different sectors of the community. The answer given is that supply and demand will always tend towards a state of equilibrium. This assumes that manufacturer and purchaser exist in a stable and 'harmonious' relationship to one another, each seeking to do favours for the other while actually pursuing their own self-interests. It also assumes that demand is limited to the satisfaction of basic needs, all surplus then being made available to those whose buying power is weak.

In real life neither of these assumptions is correct. Suppliers are geared to maximising their profits. For this to happen they need to operate economies of scale. This means that an industry must so expand its scale of production that its average costs decrease with the rise of output until an optimum plant capacity is reached. Put more simply: big is cheap! So the ordinary public has to be persuaded to buy more of the goods the manufacturer wants to sell. Long-term desires are converted into short-term needs by artificial stimulation (aggressive advertising, attractive packaging and display, promotional bargains and so on).

In theory one may still say that 'the consumer is always right', that supply is controlled by demand. But, if real needs are increasingly confused with wants, then the allocation of resources to satisfy the latter, which are in principle infinite, is not decided by the harmonious interplay of market-forces but by the exercise of economic and political power. A free-market economy, without strict political control, obeys the rule that 'to him who has more will be given and from him who has not, even what he has will be taken away'.

The basic economic problem is not one of scarcity. That is a relative question depending on the level of wants. Rather, the basic problem is how to achieve a fair distribution of wealth so that everyone's basic needs are adequately met. When distribution is made to depend on the free play of market forces then those with the greatest buying power will seek to satisfy their ever-expanding wants. In this way the rich will use more than a fair share of resources and the poor will have to bear more than their share of the cost.

Capitalist economics is based on the evident fallacy that the law of supply and demand will succeed in the long run in meeting the real needs of every member of society. It is called, in common parlance, the 'trickle-down' theory. On its own it manifestly does not work. Wealth may increase dramatically in a nation and the deprived classes be relatively worse off than before. This has happened quite dramatically in the last twenty years in Brazil. An average labourer, over a ten-year period, has had to double the number of hours he worked each week to maintain the same standard of living. During the same period GNP has risen by leaps and bounds. The moral of the story is obvious: fair shares of a cake have nothing to do with its size, it depends almost exclusively on who holds the knife.

If the capitalist explanation of underdevelopment was correct then the gap between rich and poor should be narrowing. In fact it is widening. There is no adequate reason for this except the one offered by the socialist analysis. What makes this latter so unacceptable to so many is not its deficient reasoning, nor its failure to take account of the facts, but that it implies two serious moral judgments and one moral conclusion. First, economic systems do not work harmoniously to the benefit of all strata of society. Secondly, economic conflict is wrong and should be ended. Thirdly, fair distribution of wealth can only happen when a certain group of people give up their control of economic power. This doctrine is acutely distressing to those who have got hold of the reigns of economic life. They are being told to release their grip, abandon their personal wealth, simplify their lifestyle, modify their demands – in biblical terminology, to be converted. For people firmly tied to the old world voluntary renunciation is as hard as a camel going through the eye of a needle.

The need for a new ethic

It is not surprising, therefore, that the exponents of classical market economics, many Christians being unfortunately included among them, continue to dodge the main issues. They are adept at putting up elaborate smoke-screens. One of the main ones concerns the so-called Protestant Work Ethic.

Fairly typical of one line of reasoning is the following statement:

the wealth of the West is derived not from the heartless greed of the affluent minority, or their exploitation of the numberless poor in the Third World. On the contrary, it derives from a breakthrough in the organisation of the process of wealth-creation, i.e. in human productivity itself orginating in non-material Christian moral qualities. (Alison, 1979)

Capitalist development that has led to unprecedented wealth-creation, technological advance, consumer choice and cultural diversification is made into evidence for a Christian apologetic. Hard work in response to God's calling; initiative as a response to freedom in Christ; frugality as the counterpart to modesty of lifestyle and responsible stewardship, and risk as part of the venture of faith are considered to be indispensable ingredients of a successful business life. Each is related directly to Christian values and beliefs.

There can be no doubt that these factors help to explain why northern European countries, steeped in the traditions of the Reformation, pursued so vigorously and successfully a free-enterprise system of production some time before southern European ones. Convictions like these played a major part in the initial stages of development, at a time when the fierce competition for markets and resources that characterises today's world was comparatively unknown.

They are, however, relatively insignificant beside the forces that make the wheels of economic life go round today: commodity-pricing controls, trade-preferential agreements, import-barriers, international currency liquidity, transfer-pricing, government and private banking credit policies, and many other devices whose effect is to exacerbate the concentration of economic decision-making in ever fewer hands. We no longer live in a world remotely comparable to that of 200 years ago. The Protestant Work Ethic, directed to individuals, is an irrelevance in a world dominated by the global corporation and the corporate state.

Even if such an ethic had some value in contemporary reality, we now know more than our forebears about the way economic systems work, and this has led to a demand for a new Protestant (biblical) ethic. People today are aware of the processes of rationalisation by which the mythical long-term benefits of the present system are propagated. They are also aware of the enormous human price which is being paid to sustain it. They are conscious, therefore, that *the arguments springing from moral absolutes favour profound changes.*

From a Christian perspective, the Bible takes an attitude towards the causes of poverty and the concentration of riches that directly challenges most of the assumptions upon which the present distribution of resources is made. One of the Church's most profound responsibilities today is to find a common mind concerning biblical teaching on economic life in the community. In the following two chapters I will attempt to set out some of the relative data and

6: Who cares about Copacabana?

Stark contrasts

Rio de Janeiro seems an idyllic place to visit. Even the name conjures up the fantasies of remote tropical locations basking in the sun, surrounded by luxurious vegetation and inhabited by friendly, contented people, Rio has a magnificent, natural harbour, one part of which is spanned by the longest bridge in the world. It is overarched by densely wooded hills, upon one of which stands, solitarily, brilliant white, the statue of the Redeemer Christ of Corcovado.

For a holiday there can be few places in the world with more of a romantic pull than Brazil's second largest city. The holiday-maker experiences slight apprehension as the plane glides close above the water of the bay before alighting at an ultra-modern airport. He is whisked off southwards around the sweep of the harbour dominated at one end by the celebrated Sugar Loaf Mountain. For a moment the coach plunges through the side of a hill, re-emerging to an immense beach curving away on the left. On the right tall, modern buildings stand solidly, without a break, as far as the eye can see. The tourist has arrived at his destination, Copacabana beach, one of the most renowned resorts of the world.

After checking into one of the many hotels along the waterfront, sleeping off some of the effects of jet-lag, and enjoying an exquisitely refreshing cold drink in the air-conditioned hotel bar, he decides to amble along the shore bathed in the last rays of the sun before it dips down behind the hills to the west. Immediately he is made aware of Brazil's passion for football. Half a dozen games are in full swing along the sands. He notices that the players, stripped to the waist, have skins of every imaginable shade, testimony to the diverse origins and blending of Brazil's multiracial society. Older men are fishing at the edge of the sea. People are enjoying the waves. Ice-cream vendors display their wares. Families stroll together in the early evening warmth.

The tourist drinks in the harmony of the scene, the laughter, the beauty of changing colours, the smells of evening meals being prepared in the numerous restaurants that straddle the promenade. He thinks to himself: 'so the brochures were right, almost too restrained I would say, in their description of the attractions of this enchanting place'.

But, were they right? Is that all there is to see at Copacabana? The answer to that question depends on where you look. Hidden behind the solid phalanx of buildings, shrouded in shadow, there are different kinds of dwelling. No electricity. No readily available water. No proper sanitation. No tarmac roads. An inadequate diet. The roofs will be no match at all for the violent thunderstorms that hit Rio from time to time. Those condemned to live in such conditions will almost certainly never have the chance to move to more dignified surroundings.

But the tourist does not want to know. It might stir in him sensations of guilt about the 'good life' he is enjoying. Guilt and a pleasurable holiday do not go together.

Copacabana illustrates the sad plight of human beings caught in the trap of poverty. More importantly it bears witness to the savage consequences of discriminatory incomes. According to the Bible the stark contrast of situations like this is directly due to a world that refuses to hear and live by the word of God. The pattern of life enshrined in the environments of Copacabana is also displayed in numerous examples from the history of the people of Israel. God's analysis of and judgment upon the situation is clearly evident. If we are to escape complicity with a system that allows such discrepancies in living standards, we need to take care how and where we look. Who cares about Copacabana? God does.

The biblical view of the accumulation and use of wealth

In the history of the Hebrew people it was from the days of the institution of the monarchy onwards that the accumulation of wealth brought about an increasingly unequal society. Roland de Vaux (1965: 72–3) sums up what happened:

> In the early days of the settlement (in the Promised land), all the Israelites enjoyed more or less the same standard of living. Wealth came from the land, and the land had been shared out between the families. . . . Commerce, and the buying and selling of real estate for profit, were as yet unimportant factors in economic life. . . . Between these two centuries (the tenth and the eighth) a social revolution had taken place. The monarchical institutions produced . . . a class of officials who drew a profit from their posts and favours granted them by the king.

(a) Private accumulation forbidden

At the time of the confederation of the tribes (Joshua and Judges) the *private* accumulation of wealth was made difficult. In the period of the kings, however (from Saul onwards), riches were amassed by a class of people who made up the king's retinue. This was done, first, by the acquisition of increasing amounts of immovable property (land and houses) received as a result of services rendered and, later under Solomon, through the rise of trading concessions given to a new merchant class.

The practice of slavery and the existence of wage-earners in Israel give evidence for the existence of personally accumulated wealth. An Israelite became a slave either when he was unable to repay outstanding debts, or as a security against their repayment (Deut. 15.2–3). The practice also implies the existence of money-lenders who, following the custom of neighbouring states, charged high rates of interest (2 Kgs. 4.1–7; Neh. 5.1–13; Prov. 28.8; Ezek. 18.8).

The wage-earner became an institution when some had accumulated for themselves sufficient capital to hire workers to produce for them. Most of these were forced to sell their labour as they had become impoverished through the loss of their land (Deut. 24.14; Job. 7.1–2). Almost exactly the same situation exists in many Third World societies today.

Throughout the Old Testament there are indications that the private accumulation of wealth was considered contrary to the terms of God's covenant with his people. The clearest evidence comes in the Sabbatical Year (Exod. 21.2–6; 23.10–11; Lev. 25.1–7; Deut. 15.1–18). This year (one in seven) was marked by a rest for the land, a freeing of Israelite slaves and the cancelling of all debts.

The Sabbatical Year responded to the ideal of a nation accountable to God for the welfare of every member.

> The alienation of family property and the development of lending at interest led to the growth of pauperism and the enslavement of defaulting debtors or their dependants. This destroyed that social equality which had existed at the time of the tribal federation and which still remained as an ideal. (de Vaux, 1965: 173)

The concept of property among the Israelites sprang from the terms of the covenant God made with them. It was the very opposite of that practised by the Egyptians. In Egypt all land belonged either to the king or to the great temples. The Pharoah and the priests held it in trust from the gods, but administered it for their own enrichment. A situation to their advantage was reinforced by divine sanction.

In Israel, however, kings were unknown in the early period of the settlement of Palestine. When monarchy did come it was regarded as a step backwards (cf. Judg. 8.22–3). The tribe of Levi (the priests) were not allowed to own land (Deut. 12.12; 18.1–8; 26.12). In this way God shows his people clearly that the land (the source of wealth) is to be held on trust for the benefit of every person. There had to be no specially privileged group. Divine sanction was given to the ideal of equality among brethren.

Such a situation was not accidental. It reflected the experience of the Hebrews in Egypt as a powerless, subjugated and oppressed minority. For the inevitable consequence of accumulation is exploitation.

Some will object to this argument by saying that the enjoyment of wealth is but the natural consequence of obedience to God, while poverty is the evidence of disobedience (Ps. 1.3; 112.1–3; Prov. 10.15–16). However, the notion of individual reward for a righteous life is relatively unknown in Israel. Where it occurs it may look back to an idealised view of the life of the patriarchs (Gen. 39.2–3). Or, it may be stated as a general theory in times of great apostasy. On the other side, there are plenty of protests against any simple identification of being rich with being righteous before God.

In the first place, there were some who lived blamelessly in God's sight who nevertheless experienced misery. God vindicated Job's innocence against the persistent accusations of the 'friends' (the result of their wrong religious outlook on life) that his plight was due to hidden and unconfessed sin (Job 1.1–5; 42.10–15). Then, secondly, it would not be doubted that many evil, unscrupulous men had acquired great wealth, a situation that exercised the faith of many biblical writers (Ps. 94.1–7; 73.3–20; Jer. 12.1–2). From a biblical perspective there is no necessary connection at all between the prosperity of individual people and their acknowledgment of God.

Those who argue to the contrary forget one highly important element of biblical faith. God's covenant is made with a whole people, not with isolated individuals. Where God promises the enjoyment of well-being it is for the whole nation. And, precisely for this reason, he does not allow great differences of wealth. Listen to the sequence of Deut. 15.4–5: 'The Lord your God will bless you in the land that he is giving you. Not one of your people will be poor if you obey him and carefully observe everything I command you today.'

The linking of cause and effect is the exact opposite of that put forward by those who link together great possessions and faithfulness to God. His blessing is truly experienced when there are no poor around; poverty will disappear when people obey God's laws. Its existence is proof that the people as a whole have broken the terms of the covenant.

There can be no doubt, if we approach the Bible with honesty, that private accumulation is usually deemed to be the result not of harmless transactions in the market-place, but of either violence, fraud, bribes or expropriation (e.g. Isa. 5.8; Mic. 2.2; Hos. 12.8; Amos 8.5–6; Jer. 5.28 – the references could be multiplied many times over).

(b) The creation and sharing of wealth

At this point we need to stress another important aspect of the Bible view of wealth. A very careful distinction is made between wealth created and shared and wealth used for private consumption alone. In the first case people are the sole objects of the productive process. In the second case, the objectives of the productive process are the personal power and pleasure that the creation of wealth gives.

This distinction has to be reiterated many times in order to counteract the accusation that those who believe that economic equality is the fundamental criterion of economic life do not believe in economic growth. The accumulation of wealth is praised as a just and necessary activity. Private accumulation, however, is unreservedly and remorselessly condemned, because it can only take place at the expense of others. Over against the intense individualism of many modern Christians (which seriously distorts their understanding of Scripture) God's Word sets forth the value of corporate solidarity.

One of the implications of the revelation of God's will through the Law and the prophets is that the capitalist economic system, based on the inalienable right of private property and on competition, cannot be justified as an ideal. Created wealth belongs to all the people. From first to last both the earth and the natural talents and expertise of men and women are gifts from the Lord.

(c) The evidence of the New Testament

The Old Testament case on the creation and ownership of wealth is so abundantly clear that some, wishing to evade the consequences, have sought to show that the New Testament says something quite different.

This, however, is far from the case. The evidence shows that every writer strongly upholds the teaching of the Old Testament — a not surprising fact,seeing that this was their Bible, the very oracles of God. The New Testament, I believe, presents a totally consistent attitude towards wealth. We can sum it up in the form of four major assumptions.

First, there is no evidence to suggest that wealth beyond the provision of the basic necessities for daily living (Matt. 6.11, 19, 24-25, 31-33) is regarded as the result of God's particular blessing on individuals. Jesus' remark about luxurious living taking place in royal households (Luke 7.25) and his identification with John the Baptist suggest that he disassociates his own mission totally from that way of life. His pronouncement upon the rich has no qualification attached to it: 'how terrible for you who are rich now; you have had your easy life!' (Luke 6.24). At no time or place was he in the least sympathetic to those segments of society that were economically powerful, unless they were prepared to lose what they had to follow him. God's blessing is not the cause of the great possessions, but the consequence of disposing of them (1 Tim. 6.18-19).

Secondly, there is no distinction between spiritual and material life such as might lead to a disinterest in the physical needs of others. Human beings live both by the word of God and bread. The New Testament does not try to establish the importance of one above the other. Love of God is an unreality, a nonsense, unless one displays love for one's brethren by meeting their daily needs when occasion demands (1 John 3.17-18). The New Testament balances a supreme confidence in God to supply all our needs (Matt. 6.25ff) with the command to each one to discover the needs of others and satisfy them (Jas. 2.14ff). Prayer and social action are two sides of the same coin.

Thirdly, the New Testament knows of no ascetic ideal. Poverty is not regarded as an ideal to gain some 'spiritual' end. The poor are blessed, not because they are poor and therefore cannot experience the anxieties of being rich, but because the kingdom of God belongs to them (Luke 6.20). In other words, the new order of life that Jesus is creating will mean a reversal of their fortunes (cf. Luke 1.52-3; 16.25). Only those comfortably off and wishing to maintain their privileges could believe that the poor are content in spite of their circumstances. Creation is meant to be enjoyed to the full (1 Tim. 4.4; 6.17). The only condition is that everyone has access to that enjoyment.

Fourthly, the New Testament upholds the principle that economic life should work on the principle of 'from everyone according to their ability to everyone according to their needs' (Acts 2.45-6; 2 Cor. 8.13-14; 2 Thess. 3.6-13). The inward disposition required is the willingness to share. The outward, concrete result will be the meeting of the legitimate needs of all people for a dignified, responsible life.

Of course, the New Testament writers are well aware of the profound obstacles that stand in the way of achieving these ideals. They know, for example, that private accumulation is the result of an innate tendency to covet far more than we need. Of all the sins that bar entry into the kingdom greed is the only one Paul calls idolatry (Eph. 5.5). Greed is the outward sign that money has become our all-absorbing interest. Money becomes an idol whenever it is used, on however small a scale, to exert power and influence for personal privileges and pleasure and whenever it is not fulfilling its primary object of meeting basic human needs.

'The love of money is the source of all evil'. Such devotion to gaining wealth is incompatible with the love of God and one's neighbour. When money becomes separated from the principle of responsible stewardship in recognition that God owns all things, it exerts an independent existence of its own. When money remains as private accumulation, not being shared, it stands over against Jesus Christ who has identified himself with the hungry, naked, the homeless, the sick and those persecuted for the sake of justice. As an end in itself it becomes an instrument of Satan (Acts 5.3), to exploit (Luke 19.8; Jas. 5.1-6) and cause misery (Luke 16.19ff) to others.

Private accumulation hinders a person from entering the kingdom (e.g. the rich young ruler, the rich fool), for delight in riches chokes the message of Christ (Matt. 13.22). The rich person escapes from the deceptive and seductive power of wealth only with great difficulty. Wealth displaces the centre of reality and the meaning of life from the Creator to the creation.

The uniform teaching of the New Testament is so direct and uncompromising that Jesus' disciples were provoked into exclaiming, 'who, then, can be saved?' (Mark 10.26). The master's sayings were perceived to be hard. So much so, that Christians down the ages have found what they fervently hope is an escape clause. They interpret Jesus (and Paul, James, John and the author of Hebrews) to have allowed a distinction between the possession of wealth and a right attitude to wealth. So that, if one is able to sit lightly to one's riches (not put one's trust in them) one may still go on enjoying them for oneself. Though such a distinction is impossible for humans to make by themselves, so the argument runs, it is possible with the help of God (Mark 10.27).

Unfortunately, such a belief is at best wishful thinking and at worst a dangerous self-delusion. Let us follow through the case of the 'rich young ruler' in order to be clear just what Jesus was saying. The condition for his inheriting eternal life was clearly laid down, 'go and sell all you have and give the money to the poor . . . : then come and follow me' (Mark 10.21). In his case the grip of possessions had taken a strong hold on his life. What he needed above all else was to switch his allegiance from mammon to God. 'Riches in heaven' (Mark 10.21) was incompatible with maintaining riches on earth. The absolute demand that Jesus laid upon the man is underlined in several ways in the story: twice the disciples show astonishment at Jesus' teaching (Mark 10.24, 26); the second time they were 'completely amazed' — hardly an apt response, if Jesus had merely said 'for those who trust in riches'; the light dawns for Peter when he responds, 'look we have left everything and followed you'.

My interpretation of this passage is obviously open to dispute. Nonetheless it does seem that the passage coheres only on the basis of a rigourist interpretation. My intention is that the text, at this point, may speak for itself precisely because, in my opinion, exegetes (or more likely, expositors) have sought to find an escape clause. It will be understood that a Christian's attitude to wealth cannot be based on one text or passage alone, though this one is important. I also believe that the biblical text is often distorted through biased spectacles by those who happen to have great wealth. Discipleship in this passage is defined in terms of actually divesting oneself of wealth. A rich person cannot enter God's kingdom anymore than a camel can pass through the eye of a needle. The overwhelming weight of biblical evidence suggests that private accumulation of wealth is not to be tolerated beyond the enjoyment of a frugal, adequate lifestyle when substantial sectors of society (in our world hundreds of millions) do not have the basic necessities of their existence met. The problem with excessive possessions is that they confirm the belief that a person has an inalienable right to go on surrounding himself with an increasing number of goods and services. It may be significant that Jesus did not ask the rich man whether he had obeyed the tenth commandment, 'you shall not covet'.

The answer to the man's predicament was to challenge him not to change his attitude, but to sell everything. The response of Jesus to Peter's exclamation shows the absolute priority of sharing (Mark 10.29-30). The reward for following Jesus and proclaiming the gospel is to become a fully integrated member of a new family in which things are held in common.

The story of Zacchaeus illustrates the same point. He effectively stripped himself of his private wealth. Half of his belongings were given to the poor; most of the other half went to pay back those from whom he had extorted money (Luke 19.8-9). (Four times was what the Law required for robbery — Exod. 22.1.) Jesus' response was, 'Today salvation has come to this house, since he also is a son of Abraham'.

We can conclude, then, that the economic system set out by God in the provisions of the covenant, and backed by the uncompromising stand of the prophets, Jesus and the apostles was geared to satisfying the needs of every person (and particularly those unprotected in society.)

Our present economic order — a far cry from any idealised society based on the Christian values of hard work, compassion and sharing — is basically a want-satisfying system. It is this fact that creates the great disparities in living standards across the globe.

The continuing existence of the poor is a tremendous challenge to the theological reflection, conscience and action of Christians everywhere. How we respond is a touchstone of the authenticity of our witness to Jesus. What can realistically be done about the situation?

7: That the hungry may be filled with good things

The way that we are conditioned to look at economic matters today is so far from God's will for the human race that it is difficult to know where to begin in the search for genuine changes towards a more equitable society.

Christians, in opting to follow Jesus Christ, have an inescapable obligation to discover from Scripture God's purposes for human beings living in community. They also need to discern what is going on in the world around them, subjecting every aspect of life to the rigorous critique of God's Word.

Most Christians, unfortunately, have not yet learnt how to carry out the process. The result has been a lamentable acceptance of the conventional wisdom of their respective peer groups. This can be clearly seen in a number of instances taken from economic life. In this chapter we will discuss the Christian's responsibility to promote effective and beneficial change, the problem of development, and possible ways of breaking the mould of present standard economic practice.

More than fifty years ago J. H. Oldham (1926: 26), one of the early leaders of the International Missionary Council (a body arising out of the 1910 Edinburgh missionary conference), said something which, though prophetic then and familiar to us now through the influence of the various theologies of liberation, has still to be properly implemented: 'When Christians find in the world a state of things which is not in accord with the truth they have learned from Christ, their concern is not that it should be explained but that it should be ended.' Christians who have genuinely been touched by God's grace, understand the debt they owe to Jesus and have studied the meaning of the gospel know that they are committed to a life-changing message. They may not always see all the implications of God's Word, particularly where the wider issues of society are concerned. There is still much truth to be discovered about God's will for various aspects of life. In previous chapters we have tried to demonstrate ways of looking at economic life from a biblical perspective. Now we will draw the discussion to a conclusion.

The breakdown of the postwar consensus on economic matters

The present system of wealth, ownership and distribution exacts a very high price for some members of the community. Christians in the Western world, who until recently have tended to exercise a monopoly on theological teaching and expertise, have not on the whole come from groups who have borne the brunt of the sacrifices. Indeed, many Christians in business or professional pursuits enjoy reasonably comfortable – even if not extravagant – lifestyles. They may, therefore, be unaware of how it feels to be genuinely powerless within the system. Study of the Scriptures, however, should demonstrate without argument that there cannot be real community where there are great differences of wealth.

Again, because Western Christians have often been beneficiaries of the present economic system, they have not been able to get far enough away from it to see some of the spurious assumptions on which it is based. The value of the individual, for example, can in no way be measured by his or her value in the market. The crisis of escalating unemployment is beginning to bring home to Christian consciences the inadequacies of a market-economy to meet real human needs, work being one of the most basic ones.

Free-enterprise economics is often defended on the basis that it promotes freedom and an open society. This idea, however, is a fallacy. It certainly increases the freedom of some, but always and inevitably at the expense of the freedom of others. Freedom is not an ever-expanding commodity. If there is going to be more real freedom of economic choice (both to produce and to consume) at the bottom end of society, then there have to be restrictions placed on the freedoms of those who can influence economic policies at the top end. This is one of the fundamental issues raised by those who advocate some form of socialism. The argument about freedom is a two-edged sword! Most of us exist economically on terms laid down by those who control the international flow of capital. We are far from free to decide our own priorities and scale of values.

Here an interesting fact confronts us: the apparent tolerance of the opinions of others, visible in some capitalist societies, extends to the area of private morals only. The popular press, for example, (frequently controlled by financiers), is indulgent towards the sexual life of citizens (even those enjoying important positions in society). Loose heterosexual relationships or homosexual practices are a matter of individual decision. Others should not presume to judge. Abortion is considered a matter that a woman may decide basically on her own, though perhaps in private consultation with a doctor. An illusion of permissiveness is created. We are free to do what we want with our lives, our bodies, our talents.

The picture changes dramatically, however, in the area of the ethics of economic policies. The mud-slinging at and distortion of the views of those who believe that capitalist societies are inherently unfair and who suggest changes that will bring greater equality knows no bounds. We are free to accept the system that perpetuates privilege, but not free to modify it substantially. In this area the illusion of a tolerant, open society goes to the wind.

One aspect of this reality is the belief (often supported by Christians who have a mistaken view of reconciliation) that 'extreme' solutions are necessarily and invariably wrong. We view political life on a scale from ultra-right to ultra-left, and judge both ends to be wrong. This view, however, is emotional, superficial and culturally bound. It assumes, without any debate, that there must be a more-or-less neutral middle ground from which the distortion of the extremes can be measured. What it never considers is that this central position may itself be an extreme. Once an Argentine political party fought an election under the slogan, 'the party of the extreme centre'. Precisely!

It may be one of the beneficial results of the rise in the mid-1970s of what is termed the 'New Right' that we can now see more clearly the real political and economic issues that face us. One interpretation of what is happening is that the uneasy compromise maintained since 1945 between capital and labour is beginning to break down. The increasing world recession since 1973 has put labour in a weaker bargaining position. As collective wage-bargaining hinders full maximisation of profits, the screw of redundancies is being put on the labour unions. The prospect, therefore, of labour being able to continue to milk the system is fast receding.

As a result, the way in which the working classes are captive to international capital is clearer for all to see. The delusion of the postwar boom is exposed. As Jeremy Seabrook (1982) puts it, 'The master-stroke of capitalism is to make the rich appear, not the antagonists of the poor, but the model of what the poor would most like to be.' The vision that propels capitalist society is not solidarity, but the possibility and desirability of personal advancement.

Capitalist society neither has, nor can promote, a harmony of interests. The economic system functions through impersonal market forces. The twin necessities of the system, to maximise profits and to stay alive in a highly competitive world, will inevitably lead either to a lowering of wages or to layoffs. Further, where rewards have to be distributed between loan capital and workers, both management and labour will strive to maximise their share. The New Right have successfully, though with ultimately negative consequences for themselves, ended the illusion of universal welfare through a market-economy. Though the so-called left-wing 'militants' are often naïve about alternatives, they stand out as those who are no longer prepared to try to reconcile the interests of the wealthy with those of the disadvantaged. It cannot be done. The prophets were also militants in this sense, long ago.

Why, then, should they be condemned and abused for this when Christian people are required to be especially partial towards the poor? Of course, Christians must be aware of certain tactics and false assumptions of some who declare themselves champions of the downtrodden. Fear of one ideology, however, should not cause us to embrace another one unthinkingly. Whereas very few, if any, Christians are likely to commit themselves wholeheartedly to Marxist principles and strategies, they are already committed, albeit unconsciously at times, to the economic assumptions and values of the capitalist system. If, therefore, they genuinely want to keep clear of all ideologies, they need consciously to renounce capitalism (in which they are enmeshed) without accepting Marxism.

This, at least, is the first step that Christians should take, if they are serious about the life-changing message they claim to believe in. It has now become a cliché in certain Christian circles to say that society cannot be changed, unless individuals are changed. If this truism is not to become an excuse for inaction, all of us need to think very hard about how a changed person (group of people) may change society. It is to some suggestions in this direction that we now turn.

Strategies of development: failure and possible solutions

There are two distinct areas where gross inequalities need to be broken down. First, as we have been portraying, there are the nearly one thousand million (one person in every four) whose hope of escaping from the vicious circle of acute deprivation is extremely slender. Not only have they no access to consumer goods and basic services, but they are permanently hungry, or their diet is thoroughly deficient. The task of conquering this vast sea of misery is truly colossal. It is permanently on the agenda of the United Nations, and of both the industrialised and non-aligned nations. Endless meetings of UNCTAD have been devoted to gaining some advances. In recent years we hear of the North-South dialogue. Dialogue, however, is hardly an apt term when one side is under no obligation to listen to the other.

Most experts in the field of development, whether of large-scale industries or small experiments in appropriate technology, agree that the way forward is to help the poor nations develop themselves. This is fine in principle. However, for this to have any chance of success, there must be an awareness of the reasons for the failure up to now of most attempts at development in the majority of Third World countries.

Poverty and an increasing imbalance in wealth between nations is not just a matter of some nations possessing capital resources and technological expertise by good fortune or dedication to work. There are the historical causes that we have already discussed. These need to be brought out into the open and faced. The poor nations have never been on an equal footing in their rights and ability to trade. Most of them have been colonial dependencies for anything from between one and three hundred years. Their economies were manipulated to the advantage of the colonial power. They were kept as exporters of basic raw materials. For a long time only primary industries were developed.

This is history. The Western nations, unfortunately, remain extremely defensive about what has happened. Economic development has highlighted a severe conflict of interests. Blame, therefore, must be apportioned, not to inculcate an overwhelming sense of guilt (which, in any case, is not very likely), but in the interests of setting the record straight and devising a new way forward. From a Christian perspective there can be no real change for the better until there has been an act of genuine repentance. Christians should push relentlessly for the Western nations to acknowledge the truth. This is pleasing to God. Making excuses is not.

Of course, the rich nations do have a certain conscience about the huge differences in ordinary living standards. Policies for development have been tried. There has been a certain commitment to giving a percentage of GNP to overseas development. Nevertheless, with some notable exceptions, the situation is not improving but instead getting steadily worse. A number of reasons can be given. All of them are related to the place of the low-income countries in the world economy.

First, not enough aid has been given. Some development lobbyists believe that governments should give a higher percentage of their national budget in direct aid or credit facilities. Thomas Balogh (1974: 185) believes that 'The most important task is to maximise the aid given to the poorer countries.'

Secondly, the aid given has been inappropriate. Some experts believe it is not so much a question of the amount of aid as the projects for which it has been given. Aid is often tied to the purchase of equipment in bilateral agreements. Therefore, it is used to buy technology that either the donor country wants to sell or the recipient country wants to buy for external prestige and internal propaganda purposes (e.g. nuclear-power stations, sophisticated hospitals, bridges and motorways). Often the aid is given for capital-intensive industries. Few new jobs are created and there is, therefore, no stimulus to the economy from the demand side.

Thirdly, there is an immense imbalance in the flow of capital. Aid has to be paid for. The cost is high. Interest on loans produces a situation of chronic debt (in 1970-7 this arose among Third World nations from 73 to 250 billion dollars). The greater the debt, the less credit-worthy a country is considered to be, the more it is tied to the policies and demands of bodies like the IMF. The dividends on investment that are repatriated are not necessarily reinvested in the country concerned. This is a further drain on the wealth created.

Fourthly, there is an inequality in trading arrangements. There is a permanent tendency for terms of trade to shift against countries dependent on exporting primary products. The distribution of yields from increases in productivity is heavily weighted in favour of the developed countries. (This is called the 'Prebisch Effect', after the Argentine economist of that name.) The concept of 'comparative advantage', in which each country maximises those industries in which its costs are low, so enabling it to export its goods at competitive prices, is a textbook theory as long as economically powerful nations subsidise or dump exports, protect themselves behind high-tariff barriers and form exclusive economic trading blocs.

The trend towards increasing impoverishment can only be reversed by a wholly new attitude. A real change of heart. This has to happen primarily in the industrialised nations (including those of Eastern Europe whose development aid, to date, is abysmally small). Among other policies there needs to be:

1. a *real* transference of capital (both finance and technology) through interest-free or 'soft' (low-interest) loans. This might be done by an agreed tax either on GNP or on exports – a kind of international income or sales tax;

2. concessionary trading terms, including the fixing of stable prices for primary products;
3. internal economic and political reform within poorer nations, enabling them to control effectively the natural resources of their wealth. Western nations, especially the USA, must desist once and for all from supporting, for ideological reasons, corrupt and oppressive regimes;
4. a drastic reduction of the arms trade most of which has no economic or political justification (production could be switched to the manufacture of wholesome, rather than destructive, goods);
5. internal redistribution of income;
6. a greater amount of disposal income spent within the country concerned, not spent abroad. This would help to diversify the manufacturing base of society by increasing the rate of demand.

Poor nations are not earning enough to enter the world market on anything like equal terms. The New International Economic Order is designed to make possible a situation in which low-income countries substantially increase their ability to trade in the world market. This, according to the now celebrated Brandt Reports, can only be to everyone's advantage. So far, however, it has not been achieved, for the rich, industrialised nations refuse to take the necessary steps.

From a Christian perspective a narrowly defined national self-interest can never be defended as a basis for development policies or foreign diplomacy. The criterion should not be 'who are our friends?', but 'who are the real friends of the underprivileged in the country concerned?' The ideology of nationalism needs to be re-examined. It can so easily become perverted in the interests of a mythical, ideal society. It is not the powerful nation that is great, but the righteous one. In God's eyes national righteousness has to do with defending the rights of the powerless ones. God's choice falls upon the comparatively weak and helpless.

The redistribution of wealth within one country

The second area where greater equality needs to be achieved is within our own nation. I have already argued that there is a biblical imperative to redistribute wealth on a regular basis. Ideally, this would happen voluntarily. Left to themselves, however, most people would not make the connection between maximising their own advantages and increasing the disadvantage of others. Redistribution is necessary for the sake of giving to all certain economic freedoms. It has to be done in two steps: first, through the tax system; secondly, by the wise use of the money levied so that opportunities for all citizens may be as equal as any state by itself can make them.

However, there are reasons for wondering whether redistribution is ever effective in a capitalist society. The basic patterns of wealth ownership have not been changed very greatly. The top 10 per cent still own vastly more than their percentage share of wealth. The financial rewards for certain jobs are out of all proportion to their worth in comparison with others (doctors compared to nurses, for example). The ability to enjoy a reasonable standard of living is too closely linked to the ability either to secure a particular kind of job which, in turn, is linked too closely to the ability to achieve well in the educational system or to display industrial muscle. None of these factors has much to do with the responsibility of society to guarantee a basic living standard to all people (except, of course, the chronically idle or corrupt).

If redistribution is left to market forces, then certain demands will be satisfied, but basic needs almost certainly will not be met. In the case of medicine, for example, sophisticated surgery may be developed before basic health care has been provided for all.

The state, therefore, is forced to intervene, in order to redress grievous imbalances. If it was to follow a biblical pattern, once every seven years it would look closely at the pattern of wealth ownership across the country and bring the situation back to greater equality.

This might be done through the notion of a social wage. The worth of different jobs, training and experience would be assessed collectively and each would receive according to their respective grading. This already happens, to a certain degree, in government employment. Or, it might be achieved by setting a ceiling on what any individual can earn. All surplus to that amount would be given away, either to state funds or to voluntary charities working at home or overseas, according to the wishes of the individual. This latter possibility would heighten the sense of conscious stewardship and participation in helping others.

Much economic discussion today concerns the extent to which the state should be directly involved to control supply and demand in the economy. We have argued that it must do so, if wealth distribution is going to be effective. This can be shown from experience. On the other hand, rewards and incentives for the creation of wealth and for honest, conscientous labour also needs to be assured.

In practical terms we would advocate a society moving closer to the following goals:

1. The fixing of both minimum and maximum incomes for different jobs. Unemployment benefit should be at least at the minimum level for single people. The surplus earned at the top end of the scale would be given to charitable ventures. There would be a steeply progressive tax system;

2. Every seven years the scales would be under review. Meanwhile adjustments for inflation would be made each year. Government (through a select committee or Royal Commission or arbitration system) would suggest guidelines for salary scales both for the professions and for industrial work.

3. More intermediate ownership. Wealth-sharing schemes and control of the assets of industries by those who work in them would help to overcome the essential anonymity and lack of accountability of ownership either by shareholders or the state. Nevertheless, the state would have to own the means of production of all activities that have genuinely social implications – road systems, railways, communications and primary products (oil, gas, coal and, to a greater extent than at present, land).

Much of this would mean changing the rules of a market economy. The game, as we have known it, would be transformed. The process would not be easy. There would be serious resistance from certain predictable quarters. We are all accustomed to the way things are. Often we think no other system would work. The devil we know is better than the devil we don't know.

On the other hand, Christians are already living out the power of the new age, which breaks open all mechanistic systems, all fatalisms. If a way of life is unjust it must be continually challenged. It is already under God's judgment.

Christians should take seriously the possibility that the present serious recession is due to God's judgment on our greed. Because we have not honoured God in our economic life, he has given us over to the consequences of our passion to possess (cf. Rom. 1.28–9).

In Part Four I will argue that the challenge of the poor is intimately related to the challenge of making known the gospel of salvation in Christ. We are not dealing with two separate issues, simply with different aspects of the meaning of God's kingdom.

8: A battle for the traditions of the elders?

Preaching which gospel?

Rightly understood, evangelism, after the worship of God, is the
most important activity of the Church. Unfortunately, it is not often
understood rightly.

Already, in the introduction, we have noticed how different
sectors of the Church are seriously deficient in their approach to
the gospel. In this part of our discussion we will attempt to outline
both a more complete understanding of the good news about Jesus
Christ and how it should be communicated.

We are not wanting to introduce novel interpretations, but to
recover the whole panorama of biblical teaching. The search for
something new to say, for its own sake, may betray an unthinking
conformity to what today's opinion-formers expect from Christian
spokesmen. The task is not so much to lay new foundations and
construct a new edifice, according to the modish design of an archi-
tect who needs to impress, as to restore a building that has crumbled
and decayed through neglect or deliberate vandalism.

Evangelical Christians in particular are scandalised and indig-
nant if it is suggested to them that they do not know the full meaning
of the gospel. Preaching the gospel is their pride and joy. Being
'gospel-people' is a main source of their Christian identity. Emphasising the priority of evangelism is a justification both for being a
distinct group within the Church and also for refusing to co-operate
with other groups.

Evangelicals are confident that Church people from other traditions, whatever some of their virtues may be, have to a greater or
lesser extent compromised the essential demands of the gospel for

repentance, faith, new birth and a changed life. However, they are prone to notice the speck in the other's eye and ignore the enormous beam in their own. The meaning of the gospel cannot be defined by reference to other people's lack of understanding of it. If that happens, the inevitable follows: the non-evangelical counters by pointing out the gaps in the evangelical's own grasp of the gospel. We are then left with two, or more, inadequate statements.

Generally speaking, evangelicals have a bad track-record in questioning traditions handed down to them. They easily confuse the teaching of the fathers, on which their understanding and practice of evangelism is based, with a sound, careful investigation of the biblical approach. This failure is compounded by a commendable desire actually to do something concrete to commend the good news to non-Christian people. As a result of these two factors the content of the message is taken for granted, while most creative energy is directed towards discovering fresh ways of making sure people hear and respond.

On a number of occasions, for example, I have heard evangelical Christians defend right-wing, totalitarian governments (like those of South Africa or Paraguay) on the grounds that they allow complete freedom to preach the gospel. They are usually taken off-guard when asked the obvious question: 'what gospel do you have total freedom to preach?' Sadly, the gospel that some proclaim is indeed 'good news' to oppressive regimes, for, while speaking of an 'inner' freedom that transcends life in this world, it does not in any way challenge policies that have resulted in the severe loss of civic freedoms for vast sections of the nation. Even more sadly, this gospel bears little resemblance to the searching, uncompromising, powerful message that Paul declared is part of God's weapon 'to destroy strongholds . . . false arguments . . . every proud obstacle that is raised against the knowledge of God' (2 Cor. 10.4–5).

Evangelical distortions of the gospel

In this chapter, before going on to reconstruct a more adequate view of the gospel, we need to look at some of the modern distortions, beginning with those displayed by evangelical Christians.

The main evangelical disease, then, is to confuse a particular, traditional and culture-bound expression of the gospel with the unchanging message found in the New Testament. Evangelicals often emphasise their distinctiveness by quoting two particular passages of Scripture. In one Paul speaks of the attempt by some to change the gospel: 'We have said it before, and now I say it again: if anyone preaches to you a gospel that is different from the one you accepted, may he be condemned to hell!' (Gal. 1.9). In the other, Jude exhorts the believers to: 'fight on for the faith which once and for all God has given to his people' (Jude 3).

Evangelicals, however, often make the mistake of identifying the 'gospel you accepted' and 'the faith . . . God has given to his people' with what they happen to believe and preach. This accounts for their confidence, boldness and commitment, but also, less commendably, their temptation to be arrogant and impervious to criticism.

In point of fact the gospel they preach has often gone through cultural and ideological transformation and, like a piece of clothing ruined by a faulty washing-machine, comes out as a mangled wreck on the other side.

The result may be one, or more, of the following distortions:

(a) Fideism

The emphasis in evangelism is put on an act of faith in Jesus Christ without the need for repentance, or a radical turning away from a life lived in isolation from God, being mentioned. The impression is often given that salvation is a kind of commodity gained when an individual makes a decision for Christ. The success of evangelistic efforts is measured by the number of a particular kind of response achieved by the preaching of a simplified synthesis of the gospel. This response is called, in the jargon, conversion.

Some evangelists even try to justify this one-sided approach to evangelism by appealing to the Bible. There is abroad today an influential interpretation that argues that the call to repentance was only issued to the Jews (who lived under the Law) – and not to the Gentiles – who benefited from a new age of grace. As a scheme this is neat and tidy. However, it is imposed upon the Scriptures in spite of the evidence to the contrary. In practice it leads to a shallow view of the holy and just character of God and of his demands for a complete transformation of all of life's relationships. Conversion is nothing less than a deliberate conscious turning away *from* every form of idol *to* the living God (1 Thess. 1.9).

(b) Subjectivism

The emphasis in evangelism is on discovering and responding to certain emotional needs (sometimes referred to as 'felt-needs'). The argument in favour of this approach is that it starts from where people are. It awakens in them a recognition that the gospel is relevant. And, as most people's felt needs revolve around the search for true and permanent happiness – whose content contains such things as self-identity, self-respect, belonging, achievement, emotional stability, permanent relationships, acceptance — Jesus Christ is proclaimed as the one who can produce all these things.

There is a true sense, of course, in which he does fulfil our needs, though often in ways we do not expect. The gospel, however, is about much more than the true source of personal fulfilment. It is also a call to radical discipleship which inevitably involves suffering (see Chapter 12) as the disciple struggles against both the personal and social effects of human sin. Such a message does not look too promising, at first glance, in a pleasure-seeking culture.

(c) Individualism

Salvation is seen wholly in terms of a person's relationship to God. Though this is a fundamental and indispensable part, it is only a part. In biblical terms, if faith does not involve active love towards all human beings in need (what the New Testament calls 'works') it cannot be an authentic response to God's promises. These works spring from God's love which flows into the life of a person who truly turns to him. They have to do with relationships among human beings. Faith has to do with being 'peace-makers' for the sake of others and not just 'peace-lovers' within one's own life.

A person, then, is not saved by a profession of faith. They are saved by God's grace which is appropriated by faith and whose reality is demonstrated by a lifestyle of caring for others.

In the gospel God's justice is made known. His justice is fulfilled not only in a new relationship between the believer and God, but also in the building of new relationships between people and communities where these are destroyed by selfishness, greed, fears, vested interests and obsessions about law, order and authority. This too is part of what the Bible understands by salvation.

(d) Dualism

Spiritual salvation, health and growth have become separated from material life. It is commonplace for evangelical Christians to speak (often unconsciously, sometimes glibly) of 'saving souls', as if souls existed in isolation from all that makes a person human – relationships, inheritance, social context, bodies, minds, emotions and wills. The New Testament, because it is aware that people are not isolated islands, but individuals inseparable from the context of their daily life, does not speak of saving souls, but of saving or losing life.

People can be saved only in terms of the total circumstances of their particular existence

The gospel made into a consumer product

In one way or another all these distortions can be found in the evangelistic thinking and preaching of many modern evangelicals. They seem to spring from an underlying assumption that the gospel is a kind of consumer product that has to be sold in a highly competitive market (the alternatives are secularism, the cult of pleasure, astrology, world religions, numerous cults, humanism, Marxism and so on). This assumption leads to the policy of making it as attractive and least offensive as possible in order that there might be the highest possible return on investment.

Evangelism, then, is thought of in terms of a measurable goal in which success can be charted in terms of figures (numbers of converts) on a balance sheet. There are Christian organisations obsessed by the exact relationship between expenditure and decisions for Christ. The effect of such a policy is to run the severe risk of using the ends to justify the means by making it easier for people to respond with a formal declaration of belief.

It is sad to see how easily some evangelists accept the probability that many of their so-called converts will fall away from the faith they once professed. They console themselves by quoting the parable of the sower. They do not ask whether the losses are not largely due to the fact that they are asking the people who hear their message to make a wholly superficial commitment of faith.

Some evangelical Christians may react to the above description as a misrepresentation of their beliefs and practices. It is not meant to suggest that all people preach in this way. Each distortion, however, represents preaching and teaching that I have personally heard. It is undoubtedly part of an accepted tradition among very many churches (in Latin America, for example).

The primacy of evangelism?

We need also to accept, therefore, that there is another tradition within evangelicalism that recognises many of the dangers we have listed and seeks both a fuller content for the gospel and a more careful approach to evangelism. This tradition is expressed most sharply in the clear definitions of evangelism, mission and social responsibility contained in the Lausanne Covenant.

The definitions respond to a widely felt need for a contemporary, relevant restatement of fundamental evangelical convictions about the message of the gospel and the evangelistic task of the Church. This was particularly urgent in view of the confused statements coming from such ecumenical gatherings as the Bangkok Consultation on 'Salvation Today' (1973) with its emphasis almost exclusively on salvation from the effects of sin (hunger, poverty, racism, powerlessness) rather than from sin itself.

Nevertheless, despite the widespread acceptance of the Covenant by evangelicals and non-evangelicals alike for its breadth of vision, it has not convinced everyone that it has done full justice to the biblical teaching on salvation in Christ. In particular serious questions have been raised about the relationship between the Church's commitment to both evangelism and social involvement, between individual salvation and the transformation of society and between God's offer of grace and his demands for justice, and also about the kingdom of God as an essential part of the gospel of Christ.

It was for this reason that a small consultation to consider these issues was convened by the Lausanne Committee for World Evangelisation and the World Evangelical Fellowship for June 1982. The result is *The Grand Rapids Report* (1982).

This statement is, probably, the nearest to a consensus on these controversial issues among evangelical Christians that can be expected at the present time. The result, in my opinion, is an attempt carefully to conflate divergent views which do not spring so much from seeing different aspects of the gospel more clearly than others as from incompatible opinions regarding its nature.

Let us take, as one example, the controversial question of whether, and in what sense, evangelism should have priority as a task of the Church. This is a vitally important question, for attitudes adopted to this issue betray underlying convictions about the meaning of the gospel and the nature and goal of evangelism.

The Lausanne Covenant stated: 'In the church's mission of sacrificial service evangelism is primary.' The group at Grand Rapids tried to explain more fully this rather ambiguous statement. It made two main points. First, evangelism comes logically first, for 'Christian social responsibility presupposes socially responsible Christians, and it can only be by evangelism and discipling that they have become such.' Secondly, 'evangelism relates to people's eternal destiny'. This means that if ever one was obliged to choose 'between satisfying physical and spiritual hunger, healing bodies and saving souls' one would have to opt for evangelism, for 'a person's eternal, spiritual salvation is of greater importance than his or her temporal and material well-being'.

I think two comments are in order here. The first point made in defence of the primacy of evangelism is that Christian people only become aware of and committed to social concerns as a result of evangelism and discipling. This appears on the surface a perfectly obvious truth. However, there are some difficulties. Evangelism is defined earlier in the Report (taken from paragraph 4 of the Lausanne Covenant) as 'the proclamation of the historical, biblical Christ as Saviour and Lord'. In other words, as a communication by word of the meaning of Jesus Christ. 'Discipling' is presumably understood as a period of instruction following on evangelism. The report, then, seems to be saying that Christian social involvement is dependent upon a verbal communication of the message about Christ and on further teaching about the responsibilities of commitment to him.

This assumption seems to me, however, to beg the real question about the meaning of both evangelism and discipling. In effect all the Report does is state that evangelism is primary, given one particular definition of evangelism.

If, as I hope to show in the next chapter, both word and deed are inseparable parts of evangelism itself, then social responsibility becomes part of (not the whole of) evangelism, and vice versa. If this is the case, then to talk of the primacy of evangelism is meaningless. We should not be surprised to find that it is not a directly biblical idea either. It is made as a deduction which results from adopting a definition of evangelism narrower than that of the whole text.

Moreover, discipling (if the pattern is that of the Master) is teaching through bringing together words, example and practice. Discipling, then, is not logically prior to social responsibility, but includes it. I do not think the Report has shaken off, for all its desire to see the closest relationship between the two, the division between word and deed so embedded in the Western cultural experience.

The second defence of the primacy of evangelism is that it relates to people's eternal destiny, whereas providing for people's temporal need does not. I think this is a dangerous half-truth. It is true, of course, that people cannot be reconciled to God unless they respond to an explanation of the meaning of Christ's death and resurrection for them, so that being the recipient of Christian compassion and caring by itself will not bring them into a right relationship with

God. It is equally true, however, that social action does have eternal consequences for the one who claims to be reconciled to God. At least Christ seems to have people's eternal destiny in view when he says to those on his right hand, 'Come and possess the kingdom', and to those on the left, 'Away to the eternal fire' (Matt. 25.31–46). By not seeing that evangelism and social responsibility are each implicated in the other, people on both sides of the debate can be lulled into a false sense of security.

The universalist distortion of the gospel

It is necessary now to move on to the main distortion in understanding the gospel that affects non-evangelical Christians. This is often known as *universalism*. It comes in a variety of different packages.

One of the main assumptions made is that, though highly desirable, eternal salvation is not ultimately dependent upon a personal response to Jesus Christ. Behind this assumption lies another one that all people, because the death and resurrection of Christ is already effective in their lives, will (at some stage in their development, whether in this life or another one) be liberated from sin and come to recognise that the Saviour and Lord of all things is Jesus.

In the encyclical, *Redemptor Hominis,* Pope John Paul II states the belief in the following way: 'The human person – every person without exception – has been redeemed by Christ; because Christ is in a way united to the human person . . . even if the individual may not recognize the fact.' Gutierrez, in *A Theology of Liberation,* states the same case in different words: 'All men are in Christ, efficaciously called to communion with God . . . [this] is to rediscover the Pauline theme of the universal lordship of Christ, in whom all things exist and have been saved.'

This view seems to be based on the idea that all people will one day come to recognise consciously what is actually happening to them, though they do not know it now – namely that Christ's redemptive grace is drawing them irresistibly to the Father. It is sometimes supported by appealing to two particular passages of Scripture: 'The one righteous act sets all mankind free and gives them life. . . . All people . . . will be put right with God' (Rom. 5.18–19); 'Through the Son, then, . . . God made peace . . . and so brought back to himself all things' (Col. 1.20).

More often, though, the claim that people's salvation depends upon actually hearing the Christian gospel is rejected, whatever the Scriptures appear to say. Some people think it intolerable that utterly sincere adherents of other religions should not be able to find salvation through their particular expression of faith. It is assumed that Christianity has no monopoly on the truth, for in many areas of life other religious believers have apparently shown a greater depth of insight into the human condition than Christians. As a result of these beliefs, evangelism as the communication of a message from givers to receivers is, in some circles, deplored and replaced by dialogue between people of different faiths.

Dialogue is based on a number of crucial assumptions: for example, that truth is ultimately discovered only as the result of a common search; that the only real division between different religions concerns the way they express their beliefs; that, by patient discussion, they will discover together the real parallels and coincidences behind the way they express themselves.

The belief that truth is discovered by a common pilgrimage in which beliefs are shared, as if each one possessed an equal potential to direct us towards the Truth, arises from the assumption, clearly rejected by the Christian Scriptures, that faith is the result of human beings trying to make sense of their own experience of the world and themselves.

In one form or another this kind of universalistic, pan-religious approach to faith is common in churches today. I believe its roots are embedded in a false sentimentality. Heaven forbid, however, that anyone should glory in the thought that some (we dare not say who) will remain separated for ever from fellowship with God, or should despise dialogue as a genuine way of respecting and understanding other peoples' beliefs and listening to their criticism of our faith! Nevertheless, all forms of universalism ignore two vitally important facts.

First, in spite of the two texts quoted above, there are no good biblical grounds for sustaining it. The Scriptures teach that every person, far from being on the way to God, is in fact separated from him (Eph. 2.11–13). The different writers of the New Testament use words of all human beings, without distinction, like 'lost', 'dead', 'enemies', 'guilty', 'disobedient', 'unjust', 'condemned', 'fools', 'blind', 'corrupt' to describe the condition of all who have not yet said yes to Jesus Christ. Fellowship with God is only restored by accepting in faith that God's way of salvation is exclusively through the sacrifice of his Son. This is to demonstrate that salvation is the result of God's grace and not our good deeds. The Scriptures also state that people can and will continue to refuse to accept God's free offer of salvation.

Secondly, the real element of idolatry in all religions is ignored. There is a very real sense in which religion (as in the time of Christ himself) can become the greatest impediment to a true knowledge of God (I include, without hesitation, the practice of the Christian religion). The more religious a person the further away from God's free grace they are likely to be, for they are pinning their hopes on the observance of their practices and not on the one true God revealed fully and finally in Jesus Christ.

Universalism both ignores the real condition of human beings and treats the witness of Scripture as unreliable. Inter-faith dialogue, as some understand it, undermines the self-identity of Christian faith and turns the gospel into yet another religion. As a result the urgency of evangelism is severely shaken and weakened.

The discussion of this chapter, I believe, points to a series of fundamental misunderstandings concerning the meaning of the gospel and evangelism. The result continues to be an unnecessary polarisation within the world-wide Church between 'evangelicals' and 'social activists'. Both, in different ways, are interpreting the Scriptures according to traditions they have received, but which are not those of the apostles and prophets.

The credibility of our claims and the effectiveness of our testimony and work depends upon rediscovering biblical teaching according to its own terms of reference.

We dedicate the next chapter to an attempt to look afresh at evangelism bearing in mind both the current deviations and the relevant teaching of both Old and New Testament.

9: Good news for outsiders

A change of words

We have spoken successively of God's kingdom, of the poor of the world and of the gospel. The New Testament speaks of the gospel of the kingdom for the poor. We would like to try to spell out what this whole phrase means. I believe that it is the clue that we need, if we are going to rediscover for today the task Christ has given his people.

Discussion about the meaning of the gospel and its bearing on moral issues affecting the whole of society is often confused by the use of words. Gospel has a kind of technical ring about it. It is a shorthand word for whatever I, or the Christian group with which I most closely identify, believe to be the essence of the Christian faith. This usage has led to a situation where there is no real agreement about what should be included in the gospel.

More importantly, frequent repetition of the word, together with an inclination to condemn other people not in our group – 'they don't preach the gospel' – hinders a fresh look at what the Bible actually says when it uses the phrase. Sometimes a log-jam of meaning can be swiftly broken by simply using a different word with the same sense. Though to some it may seem an insignificant change, I believe that by systematically using 'good news' instead of gospel we will begin to ask the kind of questions that open to us a fuller understanding of the message we proclaim in evangelism.

'Holding the line'?

Many definitions of the gospel and evangelism have been made. It is hard to encompass so rich an expression in a few words or even sentences. The Lausanne Covenant understands evangelism to be 'the proclamation of the historical, biblical Christ as Saviour and Lord with a view to persuading people to come to him personally and so be reconciled to God'. Donald McGavran (1975: 94), the founder of the 'Church Growth' School of Mission, says that, 'evangelism is proclaiming Jesus Christ as God and Saviour and persuading men to become his disciples and responsible members of his

Church'. In another place (1972: 59) he declares that 'the aim of evangelism is the planting of churches'.

In these definitions the gospel refers first to individual people and secondly to individual people together in a group or community. The gospel is a statement of what God has done by sending his Son, Jesus, into the world in order that people at odds with God may instead enjoy fellowship with him. As no individual can be a Christian on their own the end product of evangelism is the Church. Evangelism, then, is not complete until churches have been formed in every locality, in every culture, among all peoples and in every nation.

Many Christians would happily agree that the essence of the gospel and the task of evangelism are as the Lausanne Covenant and McGavran have described them. Moreover, they would resist any suggestion that the definitions are inadequate, because they would suspect that any further additions would detract from the central focus on the death and resurrection of Jesus Christ as a sacrifice for the sin of individual people.

Anyone who questions that the common understanding is sufficient is immediately accused of trying to slip in by the back door a 'social gospel'. Such a message, it is said, is no gospel at all, for it allows 'good works' to be part of the process of receiving salvation. It is interesting, in this sense, that Clark Pinnock (*IBMR*, 1983), in reviewing a book by Waldron Scott (1980), which was considered by some to have compromised the purity of the gospel, says:

> the question that comes to mind about this attitude and approach is: To what extent may evangelicals repeat the pattern of development that led to the social gospel in the 1920s? How long will they insist on doctrinal orthodoxy and personal conversion before succumbing to straight political theology?

It has to be said that both Clark Pinnock and Waldron Scott refuse to accept the implied domino-theory: namely, that concern about social issues will lead gradually to an abandonment of evangelism. There are many others, however, who take an either-or stance. Peter Wagner, for example, in responding to an article by Lesslie Newbigin (*IBMR*, 1982), talks about evangelicals at the 1980 Conference on World Evangelisation held in Pattaya, Thailand, 'holding the line' against any confusing of evangelism and social ministry. He defines the goal of evangelism as 'the conversion of sinners, saving souls, making disciples', and of social ministry as 'to make people healthier, wealthier, less oppressed and less oppressing more peaceful, farther, more just, liberated, enjoying shalom, more secure'. He then goes on to make the point, which is at the heart of the debate, that 'evangelism can and does take place without social ministry, and social ministry can and does take place without evangelism'.

At the risk of being accused of 'not holding the line', of selling out to political theology, of weakening the resolve of those committed both to an understanding of evangelism in personal terms only and to the separation of evangelism from social responsibility, or of whatever else people may like to suggest, I want to argue that the Lausanne definition of evangelism is inadequate from a biblical point of view. I also believe that McGavran and Wagner are operating with an understanding of evangelism which, as Newbigin says, is the result of 'the way in which our modern post-enlightenment culture distorts our reading of Scripture'. 'Holding the line' is of no positive value at all, if it is the wrong line we are holding.

The danger of condensed statements of the gospel

In discussing the biblical view of evangelism I want to begin by making a point about how we approach the Bible. The definitions we have quoted suffer from a schematic approach to the text. They are the result of placing together only certain texts which emphasise particular elements of the gospel. John Stott, for example, in his commentary on the Lausanne Covenant, says that the statement about the gospel 'attempts to summarize it as it was expounded by the apostle Peter in his early speeches in the Acts (especially 2.22–39) and by the apostle Paul in 1 Cor. 15.1ff'.

The Lausanne Covenant is not, of course, intended to be a manual of theology. Not everything, therefore, can be said in it. Nevertheless it does tend to reflect a wrong method. Any statement as short as this should presuppose a thorough interpretation of all the relevant material. It is my conviction that this is precisely what is missing in most evangelical and ecumenical circles. Both groups appeal to a condensed view of scriptural teaching. Elements that do not fit into the traditional pattern are ignored or discarded. The result is a distortion on both sides of the task of evangelism.

Part of the problem, as we said earlier, is the use of the word 'gospel'. It has become shorthand for a concept which, in practice, sells God's revelation short. If we redefine evangelism (provisionally) as 'communicating and sharing everything that God has sent his people to announce as good news from him', then I believe Christians will come to understand a different content and practise different methods of evangelism from those at present in use. The emphasis now falls on the content of the good news. What is the good news that God has committed to us? The answer to that question will inevitably determine our patterns of evangelism.

The word 'gospel' in the New Testament

In the first three Gospels neither the verb ('to announce the good news'), nor the noun ('the good news') are very common. Neither word occurs at all in John's Gospel. Every occurrence of the verb, except one, comes in Luke's Gospel. Conversely, he does not use the noun at all, which appears only eight times in all in Matthew and Mark.

On the lips of Jesus the verb is invariably used either with the kingdom (e.g. Luke 4.43; 16.16) or with the poor (e.g. Luke 4.18; 7.22) as objects. In Luke's Gospel angels announce the exceptional birth of both John the Baptist (Luke 1.19) and Jesus as Saviour and Lord (Luke 2.10) as good news. John the Baptist also preaches the good news that the Messiah is about to come (Luke 3.18).

For Matthew the good news is always about the kingdom. This is not quite the case in Mark who introduces his Gospel with the words, 'the beginning of the gospel (good news) of Jesus Christ, the Son of God', speaks elsewhere of, losing one's 'life for my sake and the gospel (good news)' (Mark 8.35), and records that, 'the gospel (good news) must first be preached to all nations' (Mark 13:10; RSV). However, in arguably the most important text of all, with which Jesus begins his public ministry, the good news is clearly that the kingdom of God is at hand' (Mark 1.14–15).

Luke, in the Acts of the Apostles, prefers the verb to the noun (the latter only occurs twice), while Paul in his letters prefers the noun to the verb. In most cases in the Acts the exact nature of the good news is not specified. Where its content is revealed it refers to: Jesus as the Messiah (5.42); the kingdom of God and the name of Jesus Christ (8.12); Jesus (8.35); peace by Jesus Christ (10.36); the Lord Jesus (11.20); resurrection as the fulfilment of the Scriptures (13.32); a living God (14.15); Jesus and the resurrection (17.18); the grace of God (20.24). Luke sums up the whole apostolic message as the kingdom of God and the Lord Jesus Christ in fulfilment of the Old Testament Scriptures (Acts 28.23, 30).

From this brief survey so far we can see that the good news is about God's activity in establishing a new order where he reigns. This new order expresses God's grace, peace, forgiveness and justice. Those for whom the coming of the kingdom through the life, death and resurrection of Jesus is good news, are the poor. Proclaiming the good news (evangelism) is to explain the meaning of Jesus Christ and to invite all who will to enter into the kingdom, taking his yoke upon them and following him (Matt. 11.29–30).

As far as Paul is concerned we note at once that he tends to use the word 'gospel' as a semi-technical term without specifying any particular content. The word occurs on its own exactly half the number of times he uses both verb and noun (35 out of 71). In another sixteen cases he refers to the gospel as 'of God' or 'of Christ'. This leaves twenty occasions where the content is specified in the context: for example, God's judgment; salvation; the promise of the Old Testament; peace; the conquest of death; the resurrection of Christ and his royal descent from David.

On two occasions the content is interpreted widely. In 1 Corinthians 15.1ff it refers to Christ's death and resurrection in fulfilment of the Scriptures, his appearance to both his apostles and disciples and to the kingdom. In Romans 1.16–17 it refers to the revelation of God's righteousness (justice), a theme that Paul develops in at least the first eleven chapters of his letter to the Church in Rome, if not in the whole book (cf. 11.28; 15.29).

There are two other occasions where Paul speaks of proclaiming the good news in, perhaps, an unusual way. In Romans 1.15 he speaks about evangelising the Church in Rome; in 2 Corinthians 9.13 the collection among the churches in Macedonia for the poor Christians in Jerusalem is seen as a proclamation of the good news of Christ.

In the rest of the New Testament the term occurs only eight times: once in Hebrews; four times in 1 Peter and three times in Revelation. Little more, however, is added to its meaning in these passages.

Even with this very brief summary of what the New Testament actually says about the gospel and evangelism it should become immediately apparent that most modern understandings are deficient. The Lausanne Covenant does use the phrase 'spreading the good news', suggesting a wider definition of evangelism than just proclamation. However, it then goes on to restrict the good news to the death and resurrection of Jesus Christ for our sins, according to the Scriptures, the offer of the forgiveness of sins and the liberating gift of the Holy Spirit. Though it sets evangelism in the context of the Lordship of Christ and the cost of discipleship, there is no mention of the new Messianic age of the kingdom.

Nevertheless, John Stott in his comment on section 5 of the Covenant, 'Christian Social Responsibility', says something highly significant: 'we must remember that Jesus drew no distinction between salvation and the kingdom of God'. He quotes Mark 10.23–7 and Isaiah 52.7 as relevant references. It is the latter reference in particular that sets the scene for the New Testament understanding of the gospel. It reminds us, first and foremost, that the good news is that, despite all appearances to the contrary, God reigns and that his purposes of peace and salvation are being fulfilled.

The gospel is the incredibly wonderful news that in the midst of strife, violence, pride, selfishness and arrogance God is bringing salvation to his people (Isa. 40.9; 41.27; 52.7; 60.6; 61.1). The news is that God has acted in history through his Messiah to establish a new order among human beings of justice, harmony and well-being. This being so, the gospel of Jesus, which proclaims the reality of a new order through his death and resurrection, cannot be restricted to the forgiveness of sin and the removal of its power from individual lives. Nor should our evangelism.

Those who accept and those who reject the gospel

The meaning of the gospel and evangelism can be further clarified by considering both those who, at the time of Jesus and the apostles, accepted the good news gladly and those who rejected it.

According to the first three Gospels the good news is proclaimed far and wide by Jesus, the twelve and the seventy (Luke 4.43; 8.1; 9.6). It is assumed, however, that only the poor will respond favourably to the message. But, who are the poor? And, why only they?

According to Luke they are the materially poor. There can be no doubt about this. They are contrasted to the rich, who have had an easy life, are now full, but who will go hungry (Luke 6.24–5). Jesus cannot be talking about the 'spiritually' rich. Nor is he speaking about the 'spiritually' poor. Zacchaeus, on accepting Jesus into his house, gave away or gave back his material wealth (Luke 19.8). The rich man of one parable was called a fool for believing that material abundance was a substitute for obedience to God (Luke 12.16–21); of another parable he ended up separated completely and for ever from God's presence. The Pharisees were castigated by Jesus (only in Luke) for being 'lovers of money' (Luke 16.14; RSV). So, the literally poor are blessed. Why? First, because they are open to responding positively to the good news about the kingdom; secondly, because the kingdom promised to them means the restoration of abundance to all, rather than some enjoying the good things of life at the expense of others. Many commentators have noticed that one of the central themes of Luke's Gospel is what they call 'the great reversal'. In the kingdom all will share equally.

According to Matthew the poor are so 'in spirit'. Is Matthew trying to 'spiritualise' the unambiguous, down-to-earth references of Luke, as some have accused him? I do not think so. He is describing poverty both as an outward reality and an inward attitude. The poor are all those who recognise their limitations, weaknesses and dependence upon God – those who, for whatever reason, are the outsiders of society, whether materially poor or not: taxgatherers, prostitutes, lepers, the demon-possessed, the physically handicapped, the violators of the law, women and children. These people in particular heard Jesus gladly, because the message of the kingdom came to them in their situation of suffering and rejection as good news of a new order in which their misery would be turned into joy and their despair into hope.

At the same time, the good news of the kingdom also provoked violent opposition (Matt. 11.12). Those violent people who try to seize the kingdom are probably ruthless political, religious and economic pragmatists bent on forcing the kingdom to serve their own ends.

Jesus said that only those who became like little children could enter the kingdom. In trying to understand the meaning of this illustration much sentimental nonsense has been talked about children's greater openness to 'spiritual' things or greater capacity for faith. This, however, is not the point Jesus is making in the context of his ministry. The point is that little children are essentially those who possess little or no resources of their own. They have neither wealth, power, prestige, privilege or knowledge. In contrast those who refused to accept the message of the kingdom and who opposed Jesus, who embodied its reality, had too much to give up. They were the materially rich, the spiritually proud, the politically ambitious and the intellectually arrogant leaders of the time (Mark 10.14–15; 21–3; Matt. 11.23–6). Until such time as they gave up all the resources they possessed for themselves to share them with others (until they were converted) there was no chance of entering the kingdom.

Paul agrees entirely with the Gospel accounts. He shared in his ministry exactly the same experience as Jesus. 'The wise, the scholars, the powerful and those of high social standing' all resist the gospel (1 Cor. 1.18–22; 26–8). All these people have three characteristics in common; they are possessors (of wisdom, understanding, religious truth, political power, social standing or economic wealth); they boast about what they own (1 Cor. 1.29, 31), and they despise those who own next to nothing (1 Cor. 1.27–8).

For all these people the gospel is 'bad news', for in the new age they will have no special privileges (beyond those of service), they will not be able to boast of any superior expertise and they will be equal to those they now despise. The message of Jesus comes to them especially as a challenge to throw away *all* their old securities.

The 'foolish', the 'weak', the 'lowly' and the 'despised' believed and accepted the good news that Jesus Christ alone was the source of all wisdom (not human intelligence), all righteousness (not the ritual observance of legal codes), all sanctification (not the adherence to the customs of a self-designated higher civilisation), all redemption and freedom (not power, wealth or education) (1 Cor. 1.30).

The rich *cannot* be poor in spirit. Their possessions are both the result of their covetousness, which is blasphemy against God (idolatry) (Eph. 5.5), and the grounds of their boasting. They cannot accept that the news of a new age coming is good, for they already own the present one, have made themselves entirely comfortable within it and have strong vested interests in seeing it continue as it is: 'the worries about this life and the love for riches choke the message' (Matt. 13.22). Only those who entirely reject – lock, stock and barrel – the main assumption of the present world that to be fully human is to possess either wealth, influence, academic awards, positions of leadership and prestige or a clever mind, and those who know they own none of these things can possibly hear the gospel as news that is good, joyful and glad.

To proclaim the gospel of the kingdom to the poor is to spread abroad the good news that God, on the basis of the death and resurrection of Jesus, is now bringing about a new creation in which the proud are scattered, the rich sent empty away, the lowly are lifted up and the hungry filled with good things.

Evangelism and social action are one task, not two

If evangelism is understood biblically as making known, both by word and deed, the good news about Jesus and the kingdom then social action becomes an integral part of one and the same task. The separation between the two is the result of maintaining a divorce between a verbal and a visual proclamation of the gospel. It is due to the false assumption that communication of the message can be restricted to the verbal statement of certain propositions. This belief is a manifest absurdity, as we recognise when we accept the saying that 'the life of some shouts louder than their words'. Transformed lives issuing in a caring, compassionate, servant and prophetic community are actually part of the good news. To offer a cup of cold water in the name of Christ, to reach out and embrace those despised and rejected by others, to suffer violence for the sake of the crucified one are all evidence that the gospel is indeed good news, for it demonstrates concretely the reality it proclaims.

The community of those who accept the king of the universe as Saviour and Lord is both the subject and the object of the message proclaimed. Paul, in Ephesians 3, refers to the gospel as 'the secret of Christ' which has now been revealed by the Spirit to apostles and prophets. The secret (good news) is that Gentiles and Jews are members together of the same body. As Paul argues in Ephesians 2, through Jesus the wall that separated Jew and Gentile, keeping them as enemies, has been broken down and one new man has been created in place of two (or three, or one hundred or twenty-five thousand). The Church is not merely the result of a verbal preaching of the gospel; the good news itself includes the Church as part of God's plan of salvation.

Therefore, whenever the Church *serves* human beings in all their variety of needs it *is* proclaiming that Jesus 'took the nature of a servant' (Phil. 2.7). Whenever the Church *suffers,* because it identifies itself with the oppressed and outcasts of society and refuses to shield itself from the suffering of others, then it *is* proclaiming that Jesus himself 'suffered . . . so that . . . by his wounds we might be healed' (1 Pet. 2.23–4). Whenever the Church places itself at points of tension in society, as a go-between bringing people to listen, understand and change their prejudices about one another, it *is* proclaiming that 'there is one who brings God and mankind together, the man Christ Jesus' (1 Tim. 2.5). Whenever the Church resolutely refuses to accept power and privileges for itself in society it *is* proclaiming that 'my grace is all you need, for my power is strongest when you are weak' (2 Cor. 12.9). Whenever the Church shares all that God has given it freely, joyfully and liberally with the poor (so 'that there may be equality' (2 Cor. 8.14; RSV) it *is* proclaiming that the 'Lord Jesus Christ; rich as he was, he made himself poor for your sake, in order to make you rich by means of his poverty' (2 Cor. 8.9).

In other words, by being the Church the people of God are automatically 'spreading abroad the good news'. Conversely, if the life of the Church denies the message about Jesus and the kingdom, then it is saying the gospel is not true. There is simply no neutral, uncommitted place outside of the community of faith from which a message may be proclaimed in order that the Church may come into existence as a second step, once people have accepted the verbal presentation.

Evangelism begins with a believing community which is involved with people either as a living expression of the gospel, or as a denial of it. It also ends there. As God's people, redeemed by Jesus Christ and showing forth the life and fruit of the Spirit, the Church is a sign of the gospel — it proclaims 'the Lord's death until he comes' (1 Cor. 11.26). Conversely, it may be a denial of the gospel, as was the Church in Corinth when its members did not share what they had to meet the needs of all (1 Cor. 11.21–2). Paul states, quite logically, that in this act the Church was guilty of sin against the Lord's body and blood (1 Cor. 11.27).

Verbal and visual communication of the good news are, then, totally interwoven as two indispensable parts of evangelism. We should note the significant fact that Christians in the New Testament fulfil their calling by evangelising. Nowhere is it reported that they thought there was a separate, theologically and conceptually distinct, activity called social responsibility. The reason is obvious: what we call social involvement they saw as one strand of evangelism. Without it the gospel could not be fully communicated.

Though *The Grand Rapids Report* continues to accept the distinctions and separations, there are places where it is clearly overwhelmed by the consistently integrated biblical position. Seeing evangelism and response to human needs as but two aspects of one and the same task seems to be implied in the following statements:

> Both personal evangelism and personal service . . . are forms of witness to Jesus Christ.

> It is the churches which visibly demonstrate the righteousness

and peace of the kingdom which will make the greatest evangelistic and social impact on the world.

To give food to the hungry (social responsibility) has evangelistic implications, since good works of love, if done in the name of Christ are a demonstration and commendation of the Gospel . . . Evangelism even when it does not have a primary social intention, nevertheless has a social dimension, while social responsibility . . . has an evangelistic dimension.

It is regrettable, but given the present climate of opinion probably inevitable, that *The Grand Rapids Report* did not quite have sufficient courage to accept the fully biblical position that evangelism – 'spreading the good news' – includes what the Report calls social responsibility, which is nothing else but the visual communication ('a demonstration and commendation of the Gospel') of what the Scriptures have to say about Jesus and the kingdom.

Until both the verbal and the visual, and the personal and the corporate aspects of God's good news are fully emphasised as equal parts of the one evangelistic enterprise, until the whole notion of priorities is abandoned, both evangelical and non-evangelical Christians will be guilty of misunderstanding God's intention for his people. Inadequate interpretation of the Scriptures inevitably leads to an inadequate and lopsided evangelistic strategy. It also helps to perpetuate the polarisations within churches today.

If the Church is part of the message it proclaims and not just some external agent for it, then it must constantly keep under review the kind of community it needs to be in order to make an evangelistic impact on the world. Part Five will be devoted to this end. Before we reach that point, however, we need to cover some ground regarding the union of means and ends in evangelism.

10: How should the messengers go?

The medium and the message

A number of years ago the celebrated phrase coined by McLuhan, 'the medium is the message', fell upon the world. At a time when people were particularly conscious of the impact of visual communication some thought it represented the very highest wisdom. Others were more sceptical, arguing that wisdom can never be framed in one sentence, however clever it may be. The truth is that it is a half-truth.

On the one hand, it expresses the fact that the way a message should be presented depends upon the medium being used. Thus, for example, the impact of the Pope's speeches varies enormously according to whether they are heard and seen on television, or just heard on radio. In the first case the whole context (perhaps an open-air celebration of the Eucharist) and the Pope's own presence produces a total effect. Within the general impact that the whole event makes, one or two phrases may stand out. In the second case, however, the communication is almost entirely through words. Imagination of the situation itself is left to the individual listener or to the descriptive expertise of the commentator. In my opinion, if one only listens to the Pope without seeing him then the content of what he says causes much less impact. In fact the message is rather thin, being repeated various times to enhance the visual dramatic effect. Clearly such speeches are composed with television audiences in mind.

On the other hand, Marshall McLuhan's maxim taken on its own is obviously meaningless. The medium in itself does not say anything. And a message, in whatever form it comes, has ultimately to be formulated in words. This is true, even when the person who receives a message through sight, touch or smell uses his own words to express it. The medium, in other words, is a means for conveying messages. Every kind of communicator, then, has to question whether the medium is a suitable means or not.

Ends and means

It is about the means of evangelism that we want to speak in this chapter. Do Christian people generally use suitable means? Means for what? What is evangelism trying to achieve? How does one relate the ends to the means?

Clearly, as far as the gospel is concerned, the ends cannot justify the means. That would be a cynical and pragmatic approach, implying that ultimate values had been abandoned. Means either enhance the message or detract from it. Jesus gave proof of this reality in his conversation with Pilate: 'If my kingdom belonged to this world, my followers would fight' (Jn.18.36). Using armed force to establish the kingdom says one thing, suffering violence for the sake of the kingdom says something totally different. The means Jesus chose to bring in the kingdom were already a powerful expression of how he conceived it.

In the early sixteenth century thousands of indigenous inhabitants of Latin America were baptised into the Roman Catholic Church at the point of a sword (the alternative was death) in order that the kingdom might be established in the Americas. In 1980 the Roman Catholic Archbishop of San Salvador (Oscar Romero) was assassinated while celebrating Holy Communion, because he had dared to challenge the vested interests of powerful and unscrupulous people for the sake of the kingdom. The message of the kingdom in both cases is entirely different. Yet, the people concerned in each case believed the kingdom was a reality that had to be made concrete.

Christian people today are often so anxious to reach a particularly desired end – it may be the conversion of individual people, or the spiritual and numerical growth of the Church, or the evangelisation of areas hardly touched by the gospel, or a more just society – that they pay little heed to the means they use. But, the means used will largely determine the end achieved. We will give one or two examples in which the bringing together of ends and means is very important. The issues, I recognise, are somewhat controversial.

(a) Personal salvation and mass-evangelism

What kind of message is being conveyed by crusade-style evangelism as a means of bringing people to discover personal salvation in Jesus Christ? The answer will depend in part on how a particular society interprets what is going on.

One point of view from which to look at the phenomena of mass-evangelism is that of one of the serious contradictions at the heart of Western society.

One of the most dominant emphases of our way of life is the freedom that individuals claim to express themselves in the way they desire. It is taken for granted that, as long as people do not actively deprive other people of their rights, they have their own right to live as they please.

Nevertheless, as 'pop' culture eloquently testifies, people are not generally treated as if they were individual people with a personality all their own. Young people, in particular, are encouraged by subtle and powerful advertising and by certain assumptions constantly repeated in the media to conform to stereotypes of what it means to be young – what clothes, music, leisure activities, attitude to parents and members of the opposite sex, and so on, are acceptable – and what their future expectations should be in terms of education, jobs and earnings. The choice not to conform to the stereotypes of late twentieth century secular society may be interpreted as rebellion, eccentricity or a woeful neglect of self-interest.

Modern society has promised so much, but delivered so little. The freedom of the individual is a beautifully adorned, well-publicised and widely believed illusion. Most people are, in fact, locked into a pattern of consumer life from which there is little escape. Their hearts, minds and wills have been captivated by the goods on offer. As few alternatives, if any, are given much expression, it is difficult to conceive of a way of life radically different. Most people are possibly quite blind to the cost that has to be paid. The price extorted is to lose any sense of the meaning of existence apart from what one owns (the opposite sex and one's own children often being treated as if they were belongings). It is young people, again, who especially suffer. They cry out for another kind of reality that they are not sure exists: respect, integrity, stable relations, inner emotional healing.

The horrible truth of the matter is that our modern way of life has effectively forced most of us to express our identity and that of other people either as wage-labourers or as social-security receivers. Where is individual personal dignity to be found in such contexts?

If one is right to detect an almost inevitable and probably increasing tendency to depersonalise people in a mass society, and if people are desperate to discover the meaning of being an individual in human relationships, then should not Christians look afresh at the whole tradition of mass-evangelism?

The undoubted fact that some people come to genuine faith in

Christ in this way is not necessarily a valid reason for undertaking these crusades. In God's providence they may well have been drawn to Christ in other ways. The amount of time, energy and finance spent on this type of evangelism might be spent in other ways that actually result in more people finding Christ. But the question of numbers is not the main issue. We are trying to highlight the fact that crusades, as a means of evangelism, may easily obscure the fact that at the heart of the gospel message the worth of the individual is stressed.

Mass-evangelism, as an event, tends to reflect and repeat the 'massification' of modern culture. The gospel is packaged as a product to be sold. It is proclaimed as a product that gives a superior performance in meeting people's needs of security and fulfilment than that of any rival on the market. Like any other product one cannot do without it. If possessed one will astound one's family, friends and neighbours.

Moreover, mass-evangelism can easily let Christians off the hook of building costly bridges to modern people: of having to articulate their faith, answer questions and persuade people to come to Christ; in other words, of becoming vulnerable to others, making sacrifices for their sake and establishing costly, long-term commitments. These are, however, precisely the things that restore true worth to individual human beings.

Finally, mass-evangelism tends to inhibit Christians from thinking of fresh ways of spreading the good news by relating the verbal and visual expressions of the gospel together. The gospel, all too easily, is seen as a set of pronouncements communicated by the mass-evangelist.

(b) The status of the evangelist

On one occasion, without false humility, Paul said: 'For it is not ourselves that we preach; we preach Jesus Christ as Lord, and ourselves as your servants for Jesus' sake' (2 Cor. 4.5). I am not sure that this principle accords with the modern tendency to build up the public image of an evangelist in order to project his personality. The latter often conveys the message that evangelism can be made into a successful business operation and the evangelist can become a business executive with all the trappings: private aeroplane, large mansion and a substantial staff.

Paul went even further when chiding the Corinthian Church for seeking power, influence and success without the cross: 'We are no more than this world's refuse; we are the scum of the earth' (1 Cor. 4.13).

The modern evangelist will often justify his lifestyle and mode of operation on the grounds that culturally they are relevant, recognised and accepted, and that he has the backing of thousands of Christians who send money to support him. He dismisses criticisms either by trying to maintain that the means he uses to reach people for Christ are only modern instruments that enable the job to be done more effectively or by appealing to Paul's famous saying that he became 'all things to all men, that I may save some of them by whatever means are possible' (1 Cor. 9.22).

These arguments are not very convincing. They simply raise and underline, but do not answer, the question about relating means to the message proclaimed. Paul's expression is wrenched out of the total context of what he said. He begins the sentence by saying 'I make myself everybody's slave', and ends by stating that 'to the weak I became weak to win the weak'.

The image of the modern crusade-evangelist unfortunately is not that of the servant who finds nothing beneath his dignity to do for others, and who conveys a message about the servant of God who set aside his glory to make his grace available to the powerless, humble poor.

(c) The expectations being fed

Implied in our criticisms so far is the observation that the means used in much modern evangelism are a sell-out to cultural values that directly conflict with the gospel. Another even more insidious danger is that Christians will be tempted to make the gospel more attractive not only by what they say, but by what they do not say.

People are trapped in the culture in which they find themselves. To survive the pressures of life they need to identify themselves in some way with a particular group. To be involved, therefore, with anything that may clash with a basic loyalty to the group could endanger its stability and expectations. This is part of what people mean when they talk about subversives today. Christians, therefore, will be tempted to present a Christ who does not shake the fundamental values of the group, in the hope that members will not have to leave the group if they want to follow him.

Evangelism, however, involves a call to conversion that means that people will find in Christ a wholly new identity. The message involves the near-certainty of conflict. Hebrews exhorts believers to 'go to him outside the camp and share his shame' (Heb. 13.13). Is the scandal of Christ being fully preached in our modern evangelistic campaigns? Are people being told that the values of the kingdom call into question many of the assumptions of every culture and that putting them into practice is not an optional extra for the most consecrated?

(d) The place of the intellect
Like the proverbial pendulum, Christians tend to swing dangerously between two points in the place they give to the human mind: some see it as the greatest obstacle in the way of believing the gospel and remaining faithful to Christ; others, as the final arbiter and judge of truth.

Both extremes tend to isolate people's thinking activity from the rest of their emotions and feelings. We have learnt, in recent years, not only from the biblical view of human nature, but also from depth-psychology and ideological analysis, that this separation is impossible. We now know that ordinary human beings can use the mechanism of rational argument to defend or promote deep-seated irrationalities (such as the superiority of one race over another) and their own selfish interests.

A person's intellect should be respected as a gift from God. It is not something to be ashamed of. Honest doubts and difficulties regarding faith and commitment should be answered. Above all, when anyone becomes a Christian their intellect should consciously be converted so that it becomes their overwhelming passion to possess 'the mind of Christ'.

At the same time, in presenting the message of Christ we should resist all suggestions that the human mind is capable by itself of deciding what is ultimately true and false in the world. The self-sufficiency and autonomy of the intellect is part of the modern world's myth about 'freedom'. Some people seem to imagine that the idea that human beings have 'come of age' is an invitation to accept whatever happens to be current thinking.

Communication of the gospel, therefore, must take into account and respect two indisputable facts: the human mind has been corrupted by vanity and, therefore, on many issues that most directly affect our way of life it does not think straight; nevertheless, a person can only receive the message through his or her mind.

Regaining confidence in the message

Many Christians, perhaps, are secretly afraid of the power of other people's minds. They feel they do not have the ability to deal with the arguments put forward against faith. Forced on to the defensive first by humanistic rationalism and more lately by the resurgence of world religions, they often find themselves apologetic and embarrassed about affirming beliefs and values so apparently out of step with modern opinion.

Yet, if the ultimate truth about human life has been made known by the living, transcendent God through Jesus then there is a sense in which it is non-Christians who should be apologetic for their unbelief.

Recapturing confidence means being surprised that anyone could be foolish enough not to believe in the gospel. The burden of proof should be on unbelief, on the grounds that it (and not faith) is unreasonable, spiritually unfulfilling and emotionally disturbing. We cannot any longer allow modern people to think they are more sophisticated in their reasoning than those who believe that Jesus is the way, the truth and the life.

Christians today face the difficult problem of knowing exactly how to move on to the offensive after 200 years of accommodation and compromise without seeking to regain a false prestige or authority in society. Paul did not seek any external support for the gospel apart from that of its intrinsic truth. He speaks of commending ourselves to everyone's good conscience in the sight of God by the open statement of the truth (2 Cor. 4.2). A method of commending the gospel, used with great effect both by Christ and by the early Christians, was that of asking probing questions (e.g. Luke 12.14, 20; Mark 12.16; 12.37; Acts 26.8; 26.27).

The only way in which I can see the *whole* Church recovering its confidence in evangelism is by learning how to integrate the whole of life with the good news about the kingdom. This process will mean discovering how any and every situation and activity carried out by human beings, and not just the usual ones used such as moments of conflict, weakness, suffering or bereavement, bears possibilities for sowing the seed of the gospel.

Where does the Church fit in?

The main point that our discussion on ends and means has raised so far is that the message of the gospel is not an abstract and theoretical set of beliefs independent of the reality of human beings who believe and practise it. Non-Christians, therefore, have a right to see that the claims Christians make about truth actually make sense in terms of the life they experience, and also transform it.

The overwhelming need to bring together the verbal and the visual aspects of evangelism raises in acute form the nature and function of the Church.

Some Christians tend to say that the visible community of people identified with the historical institution of the Church is an unnecessary liability in witnessing to Jesus Christ. After all, they argue, the purpose of evangelism is not to persuade people to join an institution or club, but to become followers of Jesus Christ. They would assert, therefore, that in those places where naming the name of Christ can mean ostracism, imprisonment or death, baptism should not be required. The intention to be baptised is enough. These Christians ask the pertinent question why it is thought necessary in pioneer situations to make people members of denominations in order for them to be recognised as Jesus' disciples.

In the context of Marxism, for example, José Miguez asks how far a person has to abandon former commitments and beliefs to follow Jesus (assuming that the atheism of Marx and his followers is a matter of historical accident, not a necessary part of Marx's economic and political views):

> When a Marxist becomes a Christian he does not need to cease being a Marxist . . . as if Marxism were a religion or Christianity an ideology. But he places his Marxism in a different context, against a different horizon, and therefore, to that extent, it inevitably modifies it. . . . Nobody (whether Marxist or not) can become a Christian without repentance and conversion. Not a conversion from Marx to the Church, but from sin to Jesus Christ. (Miguez, 1976: 125-6)

This statement poses a deep question concerning the relationship between the message and the messengers. Should not the Church have to win for itself a hearing, by demonstrating its credibility, before it evangelises? Is not the community itself, living by what it believes as a people dedicated to struggling for justice on the side of the poor, the first step before verbal communication of the gospel becomes meaningful?

Conversely, how can some people appear to say that, in order for the Church to grow by evangelising, it would be wrong to bring together separate ethnic communities, if that means they are less likely to hear and respond to the gospel? Is not such a strategy tantamount to a refusal to accept the scandal of the cross, if it appears to restrict a large potential reaping of converts? But the cross, because it is not only good news, but also bad news, is 'a sign spoken against' (Luke 2.24). The bad news for many is that faith in Christ cannot be separated from action to overcome racial, class and cultural barriers. In the evangelism of the early Church those who believed never adjusted their belief and practice in order to avoid the charge that they had traitorously abandoned their own culture to join another one. The breaking down of barriers that separate people was regarded as *an essential aspect of the Gospel and not merely a result of it* (Padilla, *IBMR*, 1982).

The two views expressed here about the relationship of the Church as a visible community of people to the gospel lie at opposite ends of a spectrum. In different ways both have defective views about the place of the Church in God's plan. The Church has to be accepted as a scandal. It exists before the time when God himself will put everything right. It is, therefore, in its essence a community not of righteous people but of forgiven sinners. No person can be converted to Jesus Christ without being born again into a new family and a new race. Though the Church possesses the life of the new age it also experiences something of the reality of the old age, governed as it is by Satan's deceptions.

The scandal of the Church, however, cannot be accepted at any price. The division of Christians into separate denominations, for example, is a shameful business, all the more discreditable for the lack of concern many Christians show towards the separations. Also, the refusal of many churches to relate their practice, wherever possible, to local customs is indefensible arrogance. Defending patterns of church life against any change cannot be tolerated by the Lord of the Church, for it demonstrates a real absence of love for those who, from a position outside the gospel, identify belief in Jesus Christ with the prejudices and power struggles for leadership that go on in the Christian community.

Evangelism, then, begins from a Church living as Christ in the world. It also ends there. There can be no real evangelism without a Church that reflects in practice the values of the kingdom.

Evangelism and the unemployed: a brief case study

If the goal of evangelism is to form new communities of disciples who make the reality of the new kingdom come alive, then the methods of evangelism must aim to draw people together to hear how the gospel of Christ is good news to them in their situation.

In attempting to demonstrate the unity of both the verbal and the visual – and means and ends – in evangelism, we will take one example. Our discussion will be extremely tentative, for we cannot point to any instances where Christians have been totally successful in evangelising in this way. The approach therefore will take the form of suggestions.

The question we want to pose is, how do we present the gospel as good news for the unemployed? Some might be tempted to answer sarcastically that the only good news for those out of work is a job!

This is partly true. Yet, the securing of jobs for individuals, however desirable it may seem to the person concerned, is not good news for the unemployed, only for some unemployed. In a situation of increasing unemployment, where many school leavers are without any prospect of a job in the foreseeable future, where people are driven to despair, aimlessness and a total loss of self-worth, where resignation before what seem to be the inexorable economic facts of life is deep-rooted, the good news would come as hope of change, the restoration of dignity, empowerment for effective action, the demonstration of solidarity with those whose rhythm of life has been shattered.

I would suggest that the meaning of the gospel would come alive in such a situation in two ways: verbally, by showing the ways in which sin causes the particular problems experienced and salvation in Christ brings the only hope for a new reality; visually, by displaying how the Christian community actually cares for those who are made powerless and suffer through the lack of job opportunities and how it can help to create changes in society that will enable the unemployed to secure a new deal.

I do not say that evangelism seen in this way will be easy. Christians have been conditioned for too long to think that evangelism only has to do with a person's individual relationship to God, irrespective of their everyday circumstances. That is a major reason why non-Christians see the Church as an institution that exists on the other side of a great gulf from them.

How, then, does the situation of unemployment demonstrate the biblical understanding of sin and salvation? Let us make some tentative suggestions. Much unemployment is directly caused by human sin. It comes about as the result of policy decisions taken by governments, financial institutions, large industries and trade unions that are based on short-term sectional interests: the maximisation of profits or the maximisation of wages, or windfall gains through speculation in money markets, or the determination to bring into being a society that rewards the survival of the fittest through successful competition. Continuing unemployment may also be the result of the selfishness of the unemployed, whose main concern is to secure a job for themselves.

Until the unemployed are motivated sufficiently to mobilise themselves as a group to demand job opportunities as a fundamental right, there will be no significant change in the situation. Those with power in society will not alter the situation dramatically, if they perceive that the change harms their supposed interests. It is sin that prevents such mobilisation: perhaps fear or lethargy, or an attitude of fatalism that holds on to the illusion that someone else will solve the problem. Unemployment is also the result of the way the majority of people in society falsely identify paid employment with work and with worth. It is the result of the modern cultural and ideological assumption that work can be measured in money terms, that the principal point of jobs is to secure an entrance into the consumer society.

In all these cases the gospel comes as good news that human beings in Christ may become free of the false values, myths and half-truths concerning personal worth, security and the impersonal nature of economic trends. In other words, the gospel is the ultimate solution to unemployment; not in terms of abstract theory that states that society cannot be changed unless individuals are changed, but in terms of showing how the gospel changes society in concrete ways through changed people.

One of the major problems for the Church as it reflects on how it may in practice display the reality of the gospel is to be tempted to secure and promote itself as an institution. The Church, then, constantly faces the danger, often succumbing to it, of gaining for itself some advantage from what it does. It may be by seeking to gain more members, or a more highly visible profile, or by justifying its existence and role in society by good works.

Christians spreading the gospel in the context of unemployment (and one could substitute other examples of powerlessness like racism, legal discrimination or educational inequalities of opportunity) must, then, be first aware of these dangers. Evangelism will, subsequently be seen in different terms. I would suggest two basic aspects: the real identification of the Church with those who suffer the effects of being made redundant or who have no real choice in the job market; the forming of communities of the unemployed who take the demands and the promises of the gospel seriously.

Identification might take a number of forms: supporting government policies that, in practice, show themselves to be effective measures for reducing unemployment; offering the expert advice people need to set themselves up in business; helping people to cope with the radical transition from a job-centred to a work-centred view of life; encouraging people without paid employment to use their time and talents in some aspect of community development; meeting real cases of financial hardship out of discretionary funds. Some churches, perhaps, would need to appoint someone to co-ordinate the work that this kind of identification would entail.

Forming communities among the unemployed to consider the challenge and hopes of the gospel would be even more difficult. Churches in Britain have little experience in the kind of evangelism that does not lead necessarily to people being linked directly to an already existing congregation. The kind of evangelism I am suggesting would seek to release the message and power of the good news about Jesus among the unemployed in such a way that they discover it for themselves. It might begin through personal contacts or through the organising of small group discussions about the meaning of life without employment. The ultimate goal would be small, self-governing, self-propagating communities, autonomous from, but in fellowship with, more traditional churches.

There are two factors that are fundamental to this whole vision. First, the ability of ordinary Christians to express the message of the gospel in ways that relate directly to the circumstances of the people concerned. As we have argued throughout this book, this can only be done if the reality expressed by the kingdom becomes the central feature. Secondly, that Christians learn how to allow the Holy Spirit genuine room to shape the response of the people to the message. For this to happen they have to take a conscious decision not to impose irrelevant patterns of Church life upon new groups of believers. It will also mean that the churches, as now organised, will have to resist all temptations to control, absorb or direct the new forms of Christian life that would spring up. The motivating force behind this pattern of evangelism is not the numerical growth of existing congregations and denominations, but the creation of altogether new communities, led by the Holy Spirit into discovering new ways of being God's people.

The kind of evangelism we have been trying to outline will require of the churches a very radical change of perspective. It is to some suggestions in this direction that we turn now in Part Five.

11: A family with a difference

When it comes to convincing people that the gospel is true, the Church is its own worst enemy. No amount of indifference, opposition or even persecution from outside can compare in destructive potential to its inability to reflect the reality of new life through Jesus Christ, its Lord. At all times the Church's most pressing need is to make its life conform to its message. On many occasions it has done the opposite.

Conversely, a great number of people have first been attracted to the message about Christ and have eventually become committed followers, because they have noticed a different quality of life among Christian people. This is exactly as it should be. Christian people are to be 'letters of recommendation . . . for everyone to know and read' (2 Cor. 3.1–2).

Christians, therefore, can never be content to see the life of their communities be less than God's open-ended, never-ending grace is able to make them. Of course, the Christian community will experience tensions and frustrations. Only the totally naïve would not expect this. Indeed some of the worst disasters in Christian circles have come about because the people concerned have been over-confident that nothing serious could go wrong in their fellowship.

Others have tended to adopt the opposite approach. Disheartened by failures, lack of growth, a narrowness of vision and the dogged determination of some not to allow any significant changes, they have come to believe that Church life must always be like this.

Both attitudes, in their different ways, destroy the Church's effectiveness in spreading the good news and its ability to bring its own life closer to its message.

If the arguments of this book have any validity, then the real test of Christian community lies in making concrete the fact that the new age of Christ's salvation and triumph over all evil forces is amazing good news for the poor.

The Church exists to spread the good news. To this end it needs to re-order all its structures and harness all its gifts. Outside one central London church is the text: 'preaching the kingdom of God and teaching about the Lord Jesus Christ' (Acts 28.31; RSV). It would be difficult to think of a more applicable motto for any Christian group.

A community defined by service

The Church, then, is engaged in serving the good news of Jesus and the kingdom. What does a servant-church really imply? Christians have often wrongly believed that service is one among other functions of the Church. The Church fulfils its mission by worshipping, evangelising and serving. Many churches appoint deacons to act on behalf of all in serving the needy both in the Church and in the neighbourhood.

Service, however, according to the New Testament, is not a function but a definition of the Church. The community Jesus founded is a *diakonia* (a diaconate). Service is a constituent part of being that particular community that has been called to reflect the servanthood of its Lord. The Son sends his people to serve, as the Father sent him. Those who claim to be children of the heavenly Father will be judged finally on the basis of their service, or lack of it (Matt. 25.44). Paul constantly refers to himself and his companions as servants of God, of Jesus Christ, of the gospel and of the Church (cf. 1 Cor. 3.5; 2 Cor. 6.4; Eph. 3.7; Col. 1.7, 23, 25).

So service is not an optional task for some in the Church, one among many to which they are called. Service is not a matter of possessing a particular vocation or gift. Rather, it describes the meaning of the Church's own inner life as this springs from the grace of the servant, Jesus. For him, servanthood was not the abandonment of deity, but an interpretation of it (John 13.13–14). Jesus' claim to be uniquely one with the Father was not simply the universal pronouncement of a general truth. It was an enacted reality. The claim was proven entirely in his everyday activities (John 13.17).

In New Testament terms service is also the meaning of all forms of ministry. *Diakonia* is also translated ministry. The primary concept, however, is invariably service. Ministry is service; all ministries have their origin there. So, when Paul says, 'there are varieties of *diakonia* [ministry]', he means that there are a variety of ways of serving both God's people and others.

To take on board the full implications of being a servant community is to break through an important barrier of understanding. Though it might be somewhat of a caricature to state it like this, for many people the Church is in practice little more than a special kind of voluntary association to which one pays a subscription fee for the right of participating when one feels like it. Before we dismiss this suggestion out of hand we might honestly reflect on the subject matter of many churches' meetings. How much revolves round the maintenance and improvement of the association's premises (church and hall), its rules and regulations, its financial obligations and its relations with similar associations? If we are still not convinced, let us ask ourselves about our 'outreach' activities. Is not the ultimate intention of most of these to ensure a healthy growth of the different organisations of the association, so that its life and activities might continue? In this way proof is given that the Christian faith is still alive and kicking.

A sense of belonging

A church like this, centred ultimately on its own activities, survival and success, is not compatible with a community called by Jesus to serve the good news of the kingdom for the poor. The Church, rather, is a group of people committed to one another in such a way that each is meeting the needs of all to hear, respond to and live out the new age that Jesus has introduced into this world. In other words, the Church has no reason for existing apart from the kingdom.

The Church, then, cannot be compared to any other kind of association. Even less does it resemble a club which exists to foster the mutual interests of its own members. The Church is a divine–human community.

The metaphors that the New Testament uses to describe the Church – body, stones of a temple, family, race, people, priesthood – all emphasise the mutual dependence of each member upon all the others. Community implies both belonging and commitment to one another. Supremely it means accepting one another as those whom God himself has accepted because their hostility to him has been overcome in the death and resurrection of Jesus. All individual members of the community, however we may react to them on a personal level, have a unique relationship to us because we and they now belong equally to Christ.

Given the normal circumstances of our lives it is hard for us to feel the force of belonging. For most of the time we live apart from one another. Geographically we are separate. Moreover, the culture we imbibe from our earliest years tells us that our greatest loyalties are to our family unit, to our country and to the firm or body that employs us. This militates against the even greater loyalty (or solidarity) that we owe to all people of whatever background or nationality who are committed to Jesus Christ.

On becoming a Christian we have to learn what it means to belong, by the direct action of God himself, to a new family. The analogy between the human and divine family is not, of course, exact. Whereas our human family is broken at death, the new family of God, with Christ as the elder brother, has an eternal existence. Moreover, the human family (even the extended family) is limited in size. God's family has no limit to it. New babies are constantly arriving. They are always welcome. There is always room for more. The parents of a human family decide on the size. In the divine family, however, it is God who decides. He adopts into the family whomever he likes. So it is not up to those who are already members to decide who can and cannot join.

All are invited and welcome

One of the most distinctive features of the community Jesus founded was its openness to all people. Jesus deliberately taught that its love was to be totally indiscriminate (Luke 6.32-6). In this way he challenged the 'remnant' theology of both the Pharisees who believed that spiritual purity consisted in being separate from ordinary sinners and the Essene sects of his time who made very rigid requirements for membership.

The Essenes laid down that 'no-one who is afflicted with any human impurity may come into the assembly of God.... Anyone who is afflicted in his flesh, maimed in hand or foot, lame or blind or deaf or dumb or with a visible mark on his flesh ... these may not enter to take their place in the midst of the community' (Jeremias, 1971: 175–6). Jesus, on the other hand, commanded his disciples to invite into the kingdom precisely the poor, the crippled, the lame and the blind (Luke 14.13). In other words, Jesus specifically turned to those kept out by the remnant groups with their exclusive membership. He expects his followers to do likewise.

The Church, as it serves the kingdom, must build up a sense of belonging and commitment among all the members of the existing family and continually welcome newcomers who find in Jesus the salvation they need. This balance is not easy to achieve. Often the Church opts to do either one or the other, or one after the other. The New Testament pattern is to do both at once. Only in this way can it be the Church.

The Church is a new body of people, reconciled to God and one another and engaged in the service of reconciliation. It is liberated from an abnormal existence caused by sin and a liberating force to overcome hostility, fear, disorder, violence, prejudice and distress among people.

The reality of the new world in practice

As a community of the new world in the power of Christ's Spirit the Church itself is part of the good news that a new way of life is already emerging out of the death of the past. Without being exhaustive, the following will be some of the signs of this new reality.

First, the Church will be overcoming the various divisions and barriers erected by society on the basis of race, sex, culture, status, wealth and power. Those who consider themselves important or superior, for whatever reason, are the least of all. Discrimination is a festering sore that has absolutely no place among God's people.

For that reason, Christians cannot be content to allow divisions that they abhor in their midst to continue to exist in society outside. The Church will be working for a society whose laws are totally free from any form of discrimination.

Secondly, the Church will practise forgiveness and restoration as the guiding principle of all its relationships. The exercise of discipline in cases of grave moral failures among its members is designed not to make the people concerned grovel in abject humility, but to be ashamed of the scandal caused to the name of Christ. Paul speaks of the need of gentleness in correcting faults. All discipline is carried out in the realisation that those called to discipline another may easily fall into the same temptation (Gal. 6.1).

Thirdly, the Church, whenever it is provoked by violence (either literally or verbally) will not retaliate in like manner. Though it may be harassed by the official policy of the state, persecuted by other groups, slandered or falsely accused of doing and believing things that are not true, it will not seek revenge. Millions of people down the ages have been drawn to believe in Jesus by the Jesus-like attitude of Christians under great emotional and physical pressure from others.

Fourthly, whenever there are genuine needs to be met, the churches will share their resources, including financial help and material goods. Whether or not Christian communities should, as a matter of deliberate policy, commit themselves to the equal sharing of their personal property and salaries is too big a question to answer here. The apparent failure of the early Church's experiment in communism does not prove that such a possibility is an impracticable ideal. The scattering of the Church through persecution made its realisation difficult. Yet when needed, and where it could, the early Church regularly shared its material goods (Acts 11.29–30; Gal. 2.10; Rom. 15.25–8; 1 Cor. 16.1; 2 Cor. 8–9; Acts 24.17). The Scriptures certainly do not recognise any inalienable right of ownership for those who acknowledge that they belong to Christ.

Fifthly, the Church will conduct all its activities – in particular its financial matters and relationships between people – with absolute integrity. Every transaction, all appointments and decisions will be made with the greatest openness and fairness possible. If there are accusations of injustice, discrimination or manipulation then the situations should be dealt with impartially by members not involved in the dispute. The kind of litigation before secular courts that goes on in some churches is forbidden by the New Testament and brings the gospel into serious disrepute.

Sixthly, the Church will expose itself unreservedly to the suffering of others. Instead of trying to find security from situations of hurt, violence, failure and helplessness, Christians in their dealings with one another and those outside will open themselves up to the emotional distress and rage of others.

Seventhly, the Church will exercise power in a new way. It will guard against all attempts to dominate others by whatever means – such as emotional pressure, the exercise of status, or the use of superior knowledge. Power, when it operates in the context of the new age, is only such when it can be seen to be accountable to the one from whom all authority flows. If it is not made accountable at all times, it becomes an arbitrary imposition of force that is incompatible with the spirit of servanthood.

The key to this new way of being a community is the fulness of love that Jesus offered as sheer grace. The main hindrance is fear (1 John 4.18–19). Fear divides, isolates and creates hostility; it expresses distance and alienation. Love, on the other hand, integrates, brings people close to one another and eliminates every kind of suspicion and prejudice; it creates confidence, tolerance and communication; it gives dignity and value to people.

An appropriate model of leadership for communities of the new world

We cannot leave our discussion of the qualities of the new community with this rather generalised and abstract picture. Change, growth and new ways of being the Church are often inhibited by structures inherited from the past.

The radical nature of the message and the urgency of making it known by word and deed require an equally comprehensive and bold approach to the institutional form of the community. Form there has to be. Freedom to change that form according to circumstances is also vital. All we have said about the challenge of the poor and world evangelisation is of no avail unless the Church is equipped to respond. What kind of structures, therefore, most appropriately reflect the good news of the kingdom? To begin to respond to this question would require at least another book. I will, therefore, focus on one issue where I believe that unless a basic change comes then it is unlikely to come in any other area of the Church's life. If my suggestions seem far too novel to be practicable, let us remember the danger of resting content only with the familiar.

One of the most sacred customs of most churches is to have one person – whether he is called priest, presbyter, minister, elder or pastor – as the focus of leadership in the local church. Many different reasons are given to justify this practice. The latest, perhaps, is derived from the management model of secular businesses. Though the majority of Christians today might not be able to contemplate any radically different form of leadership, the present pattern was unknown in the beginning.

In the early church two factors regarding leadership stand out. Both of them have a direct bearing upon the situation today. First, leadership in the local church was exercised jointly by a number of people. Elders were appointed in every church (Acts 14.23; 20.17; Phil. 1.1; Titus 1.5). Nowhere in the New Testament is there even the vaguest of hints that any one of these exercised a primacy role among the others. Secondly, the only full or part-time paid ministers were the itinerant workers (the apostolic band) (1 Cor. 9.1ff) (Kirk, 1973). Even in this case Paul waives the right for himself (1 Cor. 9.15; 2 Cor. 11.9). However, because it is difficult for people constantly travelling to support themselves the right remains.

In recent years a tremendous amount has been written about ministry. Some of it has been creative and significant; some of it little more than a defence of the *status quo*. It is doubtful, however, that the churches are much nearer to bringing together theory and practice today than they were twenty years ago when Michael Green (1964: 27) wrote these words: 'nowhere do we meet the suggestion that clergy and laity (the very terms are not only anachronisms, but distortions of the New Testament position) have realms into which the other is not permitted to venture.'

In fact the necessity of upholding the distinction that Michael Green calls a distortion, and thus of finding a role for the clergy, stifles at birth all fresh thinking and experimentation regarding ministry. Every major Church document that tries to define ministry jumps quickly from the New Testament concept of the ministry of the whole body and of every member to the specialised ministry of bishops, elders and deacons (e.g. ARCIC, 1982; Lima, 1982: 20f).

I suspect that even when many today speak fervently and piously of an every-member ministry, they are thinking clearly of a two-tier system: the ministry of the people being subordinate to and dependent upon the ordained ministry.

There has been a standard reaction to the criticism that the present practice of ministry is far-removed from that of the New Testament. It is argued that the patterns of ministry discernible in the New Testament are so fluid that no one particular form can be deduced with certainty. Consequently, the Church is at liberty to adapt patterns to new circumstances.

This, however, is precisely what does not happen. Abandoning any kind of norm from the apostolic era the Church imposes a norm derived from another age: either that of the sub-apostolic Church of the second century or that of the Reformation. It has been demonstrated over and over again that the threefold or twofold orders of ministry are contingent and historically determined. No fundamental theological principle is at stake, if they were to be substantially modified. Nevertheless, there seems to be precious little chance that major changes will come.

One is driven to the conclusion, therefore, that the present pattern of ministry is a sacred cow that cannot be touched. All we get is minor tinkering with the same system (such as assistant pastoral ministries), which, like all tinkering, reinforces the *status quo*. (Perhaps in this case we have now a three-tier system.) Suspicion forces one to conclude that the Church is reacting no differently from any secular organisation. Those who hold authority and status will not willingly give it up. As long as the 'clergy' have the right of veto over any genuine change they are not likely to commit suicide.

Many will argue that, in any case, the present systems have proved themselves the best over long periods of time in a wide variety of circumstances. Clearly, that is an unproven assumption; it merely begs the question. Not all that is hallowed by tradition, however venerable, is sacred. The major question does not concern the past, but the present and the future: is the present pattern of leadership the best available to enable the community to represent the kingdom and spread the good news?

I believe the evidence demonstrates that the traditional pattern is now stifling the Spirit's freedom to take the Church into new paths of commitment. We will try to give adequate reasons for making this rather sweeping assertion, though we can only do it in the briefest possible fashion.

Under the present system leadership in local churches is not truly indigenous. The one ultimately invested with leadership responsibility comes into a situation from outside, lives there for a few years and moves on. He is then replaced by another non-indigenous leader. His leadership, moreover, is exercised by virtue of his belonging to a professional class — the clergy. His gifts have not been discovered and recognised by the people among whom he works in any meaningful sense. He comes stamped with all the aura of professionalism – special selection, special training and ordination. The kind of qualifications a clergyman needs under the present system to be in charge of a local congregation are not necessarily the same as the ones the New Testament recognises for leadership.

Most denominations do not allow local churches to operate fully unless there is a professional clergyman in authority, even if he has to divide his time among several congregations. To describe his relationship to the Body of Christ we use such anachronistic phrases as 'he has the cure of souls' and 'he has a living'.

The result of the present pattern of leadership is very simple. It stifles the mature flowering of the leadership gifts among the whole people of God. Much is being said today (often by ordained clergy) about shared leadership. One wonders, however, how deep the reflection has gone concerning the practice of sharing. Whatever the theory, the reality is that leadership is shared on conditions allowed by *the* leader professionally recognised in virtue of his 'orders'. Sharing can only be genuine, however, if the people of God are free to develop their own patterns of ministry.

Observation over many years in different cultures and churches of the way the two-tier system of ministry operates has forced me to conclude that leadership under the guidance of the Spirit will never truly flourish until authority for the life of the local church is vested in the hands of the local 'lay' people. *This can only happen when full-time pastors who have made ordination into a career are no longer appointed to local churches.* Such a step, however, should only be taken after adequate preparation and training of the congregations to assume all leadership responsibilities themselves by appointing proven people from their midst have been made.

As we have said, it is often argued (again usually by the clergy) that the New Testament gives us little guidance about concrete patterns of ministry. The conclusion drawn is that the Church is free to adopt its own. This is a beguiling half-truth. There are two obvious responses. First, the Church in practice is not free at all. It is saddled with a system that is beyond the present imagination of most people to change fundamentally. The freedom, therefore, is purely theoretical. Secondly, the variety of patterns of ministry in the New Testament may not be nearly as great as is often assumed. I believe that the plural nature of leadership in every church, without exception, is highly significant. It is not simply an accident of history. The hierarchical structure of leadership that apparently developed some years after the apostles had died has contributed to turning the radical message of the kingdom into just another religion. As Michael Harper (1977: 25) says:

> The work of Christ marked the death of all religious systems including the Jewish. . . . Christians had a mission to go out into the world. . . . To do this they were freed from the baggage of religion, empowered by their faith and the Spirit. Instead, with the creation of a special priestly class possessed of hierarchical authority, Christians have built the most elaborate religious system yet seen on earth and are imprisoned in it.

The real tragedy of our present system is that the gospel has been converted into a religious way of life instead of being an agent to transform the old age into a new way of life. Like all religions, Christianity has needed its priestly class to perform priestly functions. The kind of gospel about which the Scriptures talk will only be recovered when the 'priestly' class (whatever name they bear) disappear again.

A possible pattern for the future

To recognise the problem and to counteract any attempt to erect a theological smoke-screen does not unfortunately change the situation. Something more has to be done. It is necessary to suggest and then to experiment with an alternative model of ministry. To attempt to elaborate such a model here would take too much space. I can only suggest that as the full-time, professional ministry gradually disappears from the local church the itinerant ministry of some for the sake of all should be strengthened and refocused. I personally believe that the pattern of the apostolic band is still valid. A small team of people, working under the over-all direction of a bishop (or equivalent), would provide for the local churches a support group to help in training and counselling. Each member of the team would be active in a local church, though not necessarily as part of the leadership team there. The bishop's main task would be the pastoral care of the leadership of the local churches. He would also be involved with them in planning ahead the work and strategy of the congregation. In his team he would have people with specialist experience in different areas: young people's work, counselling, education, the overseas Church, liaison with local government and social services, race relations, and so on. They would be available to the local churches when needed. They would also act as links between the churches.

The picture of the 'omni-competent' clergymen is like a tragi-comic farce. His position requires him to fulfil a certain role. That role gives him the generally accepted right to direct and manage the ministry and witness of his whole church. He also can exercise a power of veto over the initiatives that others may want to take. Only by developing a genuinely plural leadership at both the local and regional levels can the God-given gifts and experiences of all come to the fore.

To say that the re-ordering of Church life along these lines would release an amazing potential for growth is not to state an impossible, theoretical ideal. Already among grassroots communities of different kinds a new way of being the Church is taking place (Kirk, 1983). They are demonstrating, beyond any shadow of doubt, that a thorough renewal of traditional patterns of Church life is possible and that, as a result, the Church is being more effective as an agent of the gospel.

A recovery of true biblical evangelism is probably dependent upon churches discovering for themselves a genuinely different pattern of leadership. Otherwise, the Church will continue to live out its existence as a religious society dedicated to promoting itself. Both the challenge of the times we live in and the task that the risen Lord has laid upon his people point to far-reaching changes.

Moving the furniture around is not an adequate response. The house itself needs to be redesigned.

Substantial change is a painful business. Deeply entrenched patterns of authority, power and dominance can only be altered, if God's people are willing to go through a period of travail together. We all naturally shrink from this calling. Following Jesus closely in a life of obedience makes it inevitable. In our final chapter we will discuss the nature of suffering, the reasons why Christians will experience it and the subtle ways we all seek to avoid it. Suffering and representing and spreading abroad the good news of the kingdom to the poor are inextricably linked.

12: Through suffering to the kingdom

Although it might appear a thorough contradiction, Christian people who suffer for their faith are a sign that a new age is dawning. The first-century Church expected to suffer. Paul informed the new Christians of Asia Minor that the kingdom of God could only be enjoyed in its completeness through suffering (Acts 14.22). Later, he praised the Christians in Thessalonica because they remained steadfastly faithful to their convictions through persecution and affliction. They showed themselves in this way to be worthy of the kingdom for which they were suffering (1 Thess. 2.14; 2 Thess. 1.4–5).

In trying to deal with the question of suffering we touch a very deep mystery. To enter comprehensively into the problem is beyond the scope of this chapter. I will limit myself to discussing the way Scripture understands suffering, and the way Christians may suffer today and how this is evidence for the new world.

A rational approach is not enough

The reality of suffering could be tackled as a philosophical or moral problem. How can the Creator of the universe be good and full of love, if suffering (particularly of the innocent) on the scale we know it apparently continues unchecked? How is it that those who deliberately choose to use violence on others to gain their own selfish ends actually seem to prosper in this life? What is the connection between personal responsibility for sin and suffering? Is the suffering of emotional distress, for example, largely the fault of the individuals concerned or the result of their circumstances (home background, schooling, the kind of friends they have)?

These questions are very important. They often cause considerable personal concern. Though many people have tried to explain the reasons why evil continues to destroy and maim human lives, bringing grief, distress and an often unbearable burden of pain, no totally satisfactory rational explanation has ever been devised. Evil and suffering are so deeply embedded in our total experience of life that it is doubtful whether the mind alone could begin to encompass so vast a reality. Indeed, by trying to remove suffering from the profound feelings and emotions that it provokes in order to turn it into an intellectual problem, one of the main keys to understanding it as a human phenomenon is lost, namely that of solidarity in suffering.

It is not surprising, therefore, that the Bible, although it does address itself to the philosophical and moral questions, does not concentrate on a purely rational approach. In the Book of Job, for example, the easy, stereotyped answers of Job's friends to his suffering are dismissed as ignorant, empty words. They argued that suffering comes to individuals as the direct result of some evil thing they have done. Theirs was the conventional wisdom of those who suppose that suffering must be the judgment of God, or of fate, for some particular crime committed. The opinion of Job's friends is categorically refuted. Jesus also throws his authority against a simple identification of sin and suffering (John 9.3).

The suffering of Jesus is the key to all suffering

In trying to relate to the considerable suffering they experienced, the early Church began from the fact of Jesus' crucifixion. Here was the only person in the entire history of the world who suffered and yet was entirely innocent of any evil (1 Pet. 3.18). A Christian, then, looks at the reality of suffering from the vantage-point of Jesus who, though he was guilty of no crime, though he went everywhere delivering people from fear, oppression and ignorance (Acts 10.38), and though he was God's Son, was tortured to death.

The meaning of suffering in all ages is found in the reasons why Jesus had to suffer. There are many. We will briefly mention three. Jesus suffered death as a prophet, as a priest and as a sacrificial lamb.

(a) No prophet is acceptable

Jesus likens his death to that of the prophets when he says, 'it is not right for a prophet to be killed anywhere except in Jerusalem' (Luke 13.33). He accuses the religious leaders of his day of being implacably opposed to God's prophets (Matt. 23.29–37). The prophet's task is to make plain what is going on in society. He calls a spade a spade. His word is God's word, because, unlike that of the false prophets, it is not ambiguous and allows no excuses. He does not try to find soft words and nuances to describe the stark reality of injustice and oppression. The prophet addresses his word directly to the leaders of society, they are both responsible for the way things are and are able to change them. He does not allow them to blame some third party or some abstract entity like 'world economic recession', 'international communism', or 'the imperialist West'. He turns to the people involved and says 'you, and you and you . . . are the man!' (cf. 2 Sam. 12.7).

Jesus suffered as a prophet, because he challenged the way power was being employed. In particular he challenged the use made of God and religion to divide human beings into those who know all about life and those who are ignorant; to justify the economic exploitation of the poor by the rich, in particular that of the Sadducees whose commercial dealings in the temple were nothing less than extortion; to rely on force and violence to maintain a stability that favoured only a privileged few.

Like the prophets in the Old Testament Jesus saw clearly and denounced passionately the intimate connection between religion, politics and gross economic inequalities. For the leaders of his day – Pharisees, Sadducees and Herodians – he was a thoroughly subversive figure, for he both exposed the ideological use being made of God's Word for the defence of privilege and offered in its place an alternative interpretation of God's purposes.

It is not surprising, therefore, that the High Priest devised a plan to do away with him; nor that this plan was thoroughly pragmatic and expedient. How significant that the leaders saw that the ultimate threat to their power and authority was that 'everyone will believe in him' (John 11.48). Unlike John the Baptist, also a prophet, Jesus was not 'a voice crying in the wilderness'. Rather, he was someone who began to form a new kind of community, a community made up largely of those suffering from the deeds of people who wielded power in society.

Jesus represented a dangerous movement at the grassroots level, one that obstinately refused to accept the official religious and political philosophy of those who defended the continuity of a society divided into those who made the decisions and those who obeyed.

All that Jesus did and said provoked anger and resentment. He stirred up in those he denounced powerful feelings of hostility and the desire for revenge. In order to get rid of him they practised lies, deceit and violence. They were prepared, ultimately, to break the very law they claimed to uphold in order to remove the one who disturbed their peace. Finally, in playing their last trump-card before Pontius Pilate, they compounded the enormity of their

actions by blaspheming against the living God, declaring that they
had 'no king but Caesar' (John 19.15; cf. 1 Sam. 8.7–8).

(b) A high priest able to sympathise

Secondly, Jesus suffered as a priest on behalf of his people. Jesus
suffered in order to experience in every detail (except personal sin)
the consequences of evil in the world.

In the New Testament the Letter to the Hebrews in particular
makes some remarkable statements about the meaning of Jesus'
suffering. It speaks of God making Jesus 'perfect through suffering'
(Heb. 2.10); of Jesus 'learning obedience through his suffering'
(Heb. 5.8). The suffering he went through was neither a mistake,
nor something better avoided, nor a side-issue, nor even a dark,
negative experience.

The salvation Jesus has made possible is made complete only
through suffering. The author of Hebrews gives two reasons for
speaking in this way about Jesus' suffering. First, the salvation that
he achieves is the outcome of his triumph over evil. He destroys
'the Devil, who has the power over death' (Heb. 2.14); he sets 'free
those who were slaves all their lives because of their fear of death'
(Heb. 2.15), and he makes 'expiation for the sins of the people'
(Heb. 2.17; RSV). Evil, in its turn, is the cause of the suffering
Jesus experienced. He 'tasted death' (Heb. 2.9), which brings the
kind of suffering experienced by those who cannot shake themselves
free of fear (Heb. 2.15; 5.7). Death is a formidable enemy of human
beings. It is cruel, brings misery, causes despair and grief. Jesus'
suffering demonstrates that his salvation deals with the problem of
evil in all its forms.

Secondly, through suffering Jesus identifies himself wholly with
human life. He not only tasted death, but did so, in order that 'he
should stand for us all' (Heb. 2.9; NEB). He became 'like his brothers
in every way' (Heb. 2.17), so that he could represent children of
flesh and blood (Heb. 2.14) before God. 'For since he himself has
passed through the test of suffering, he is able to help those who
are meeting their test now' (Heb. 2:18; NEB). Jesus, the writer says
quite explicitly, is able to feel sympathy with our weaknesses
because he has already passed through every conceivable temptation and testing himself (Heb. 4.15). Today we might use the term
solidarity to describe God's action in becoming a real human being.
God does not ignore the overwhelming reality of suffering, nor does
he pretend it is unreal, nor does he abandon us to face it stoically

alone. He experiences it from within, just as we do, in a physical, emotional and intellectual way.

God's answer to suffering is not to wipe it out by a fiat from above. Rather he experiences it from below at its very worst. He goes through with it, passing on to a place of joy and hope, in the knowledge that it no longer exists for ever.

(c) Sacrificed to take away sin
Thirdly, Jesus suffered as a sacrificial lamb. His suffering was not just the endurance of pain, nor just voluntary submission to violence, nor just solidarity with fellow human beings. Through suffering Jesus liberated people from the burden of guilt, shame and oppression that sin brings. In the moment of crucifixion, the totality of evil became concentrated upon this one human being. He 'carried our sins in his body to the cross' (1 Pet. 2.24). Sin and its consequences were dealt with once for all, totally and finally. So, 'he himself took our sickness and carried away our diseases' (Matt. 8.17).

Not only in the act of dying, but in all the events leading up to it, Jesus bore the effects of sin. He was insulted, abused, beaten, rejected, lied about. The result is that we are healed, restored, forgiven, brought into fellowship through his sufferings (1 Pet. 2.22–5). The suffering of Jesus as the lamb of God who takes away the sin of the world (John 1.29) is the prelude to a great time of celebration. Suffering is real. It is not, however, the ultimate reality. 'Our Passover Festival is ready, now that Christ, our Passover lamb, has been sacrificed. Let us celebrate our Passover, then' (1 Cor. 5.7–8). The time for grief, tears and pain, like the thick, dark clouds and driving rain of a fierce storm, is passing over. Jesus has borne everything that we may have to bear, and infinitely more.

Suffering as followers of Jesus

The crucifixion, then, is the place to which and from which Christians go as they seek to understand how suffering can make sense in practical terms. There can be no reason to suppose that Christian people in this life will escape suffering. I do not mean just the suffering that may come to anyone, because of starvation, physical or mental disability, acts of aggression, unjust imprisonment, the sudden death of a close member of the family, or for any other reason. All these causes of suffering are deeply felt experiences. The Christian, however, may well also suffer because he is a Christian (1 Pet. 4.16).

The early Christians experienced suffering 'for the name'. For them it was inevitable (Acts 9.16). It was also a cause for rejoicing, because it meant that the world was taking seriously their commitment to Jesus (Acts 5.41). Over and over again Jesus' disciples speak of sharing in the sufferings of Christ (e.g. Phil. 3.10; Col. 1.24; 1 Pet. 4.13; 2 Cor. 1.6). They see this as a necessary step before attaining the fullness of the new age that Jesus promises. Indeed, Paul seems to make enjoyment of all that God promises conditional upon suffering: 'we are God's heirs and Christ's fellow-heirs, if we share his sufferings now in order to share his splendour hereafter' (Rom. 8.17, NEB; also Phil. 3.10; 2 Thes. 1.5; 2 Tim. 2.12).

Suffering comes to Christians because they are identified with the prophetic and priestly ministries of Jesus. 'No slave is greater than his master. If they persecuted me, they will persecute you too' (John 15.20). Power and the struggle for power have not altered significantly across the centuries. Though the balance between political centralisation, economic accumulation and religious ideologies varies from place to place, the reality of each supporting and strengthening the others is plainly visible, to differing degrees, in every nation upon earth.

Moreover, false prophets abound. They can be known by their hostility to the true prophets of God who unmask those who do the bidding of 'the rulers, authorities and cosmic powers of this dark age' (Eph. 6.12). False prophets are particularly manifest today as those who applaud and defend the policies and interests of their respective governments in spite of the damage the latter cause to those too powerless to have a voice that can be heard.

All that happened to Jesus is likely to happen to his followers. They will be rejected, treated with contempt, reviled, slandered, discriminated against, have their freedom taken away, falsely accused, physically abused and killed. Christians are signs of the new world precisely because they suffer this kind of treatment on account of the uncompromising stand they take against every type of regime which sows death and destruction.

The hostile reaction Christians provoke, even from others who call themselves Christians, and the faith, hope and love they display towards their persecutors are part both of the struggle and the triumph in which Christ was and is engaged: 'by means of my physical sufferings I am helping to complete what still remains of Christ's sufferings on behalf of his body, the church' (Col. 1.24). The cross that the disciple is to take hold of, without which he cannot be a true follower, is the abuse Christ received for exposing both the corruption of power and the deceit that religion may cover up.

Persecution, then, is an intimate part of belonging to the kingdom Jesus has begun. It is as strong a sign of the reality of reconciliation with God as is humility, mercy, purity, peace-making and right relationships (Matt. 5.3–12).

Avoiding the stigma of Jesus

Spreading abroad the good news of Jesus will result in being marked by the scandal of Jesus. The scandal, however, is itself part of the good news (Luke 21.12–15). But those who seek to avoid the scandal *of* Jesus will end up by being a scandal *to* Jesus and a stumbling-block to the poor who may want to believe in him: 'whoever tries to save his own life will lose it; whoever loses his life will save it' (Luke 17.33).

To seek to escape from suffering, even for the name, is perfectly natural. No one looks for pain and discomfort. It is easy, therefore, to find all kinds of reasons for stepping aside from the ultimate conflict that may lead to imprisonment, the loss of civil rights (such as freedom to travel), physical abuse or ostracism from former friends, colleagues and relatives.

The processes at work are often subtle. We may not be aware how our attitudes and actions sometimes compromise central elements of the gospel. Though there are numerous ways in which we may deceive ourselves about our faithfulness to Jesus, two in particular stand out.

(a) Peace where there is no peace

First, the message we proclaim may be so innocuous that it does not stir anyone to opposition or resentment. By concentrating on the individual nature of salvation and the personal dimension of sin, of which a person needs to repent in order to be restored to friendship with God, the messenger of the gospel may avoid any direct confrontation with society as a whole.

If a Christian or a church is convinced that its task is wholly fulfilled when it offers a message of sins forgiven to individuals and seeks to integrate them into the fellowship of others who believe the same things then the state is likely to leave them alone. If, moreover, the kind of unsatisfactory situation from which people are to be liberated is marked by the vices normally associated with a middle-class lifestyle (e.g. sexual liberty, excessive drinking, over-indulgent spending on oneself, dishonesty in business, stress caused by a single-minded ambition to succeed) then the Church is unlikely to be persecuted. It has effectively reduced the gospel to that area of life about which, by general consensus, the state has no concern. Faith has been thoroughly 'privatised'.

There is actually a twist in the tail. Not only does the state not intervene to hinder this kind of religion, it may actively support it. It is, for example, no secret that certain Central American governments have made available stadiums free of charge to certain evangelists. They are confident that the preaching will redound to their own political benefit. For one thing, they will argue strongly and persuasively that there is complete freedom to practise and propagate the Christian faith in their country. This is an important point to be able to make when they are being accused by world opinion of curtailing and suppressing civil liberties.

And yet in these same countries Christians, both Protestants and Catholics, are suffering martyrdom at the hand of the self-same authorities. How convenient, then, for the regime to be able to set one group of Christians against another and accuse those who are suffering of bringing it upon themselves by their deliberately subversive activity towards the state. What is at stake is the content and consequences of the gospel itself: does it have implications, beyond personal relationships, to the way power is exercised in society as a whole or not?

(b) Submit to the governing authorities, and all that

This takes us to the second way in which Christians have avoided suffering. They take a supposedly submissive attitude to the state and the laws it makes, basing themselves on what appears to be the obvious meaning of an important passage of Scripture: 'everyone must obey the state authorities, because . . . the existing authorities have been put there by God. Whoever opposes the existing authority opposes what God has ordered; and anyone who does so will bring judgment on himself' (Rom. 13:1-2).

This statement by Paul seems crystal clear. The reason, then, for keeping out of political matters seems highly plausible. Those who suffer because of opposition to the policies of a particular government are not suffering for the name, but because of their ideological bias. How easy the world seems to be when the issues have been simplified in this way! The simple, however, easily gives way to the simplistic. Shallow is precisely the judgment reserved for the belief that the gospel has nothing to do with political life.

A detailed study of what Paul said in Romans and what he meant about the relationship between Christians and the political authorities is not possible here. Nevertheless, one or two points can be made to show that an unthinking compliance with everything the state may demand is not what Paul was talking about.

The word Paul uses is not the usual one for obey. Many translations put the word submit instead. In all normal circumstances a Christian will submit to those with authority to govern in those matters that God has placed in their hands: upholding what is right, punishing evil-doing and collecting taxes for the common good. Some Christians may be tempted to interpret their liberty in Christ as freedom from the constraints imposed by living in society. They may be inclined to believe that now, because they belong to a new world, they are a law to themselves. Paul declares that this is a wrong conclusion to draw. Although the power and authority of the state ultimately will cease to exist, for the moment it fulfils God's purposes. Anarchy is not the Christian answer to totalitarianism.

The Scriptures as a whole, however, do not enjoy blind obedience. Quoting Romans 13, as if it were the only teaching on the subject, is a symptom of that tendency that makes much of those passages which happen to support a point of view we find convenient. The Scriptures acknowledge in many places the obvious fact that obedience to human authorities will often conflict with obedience to God. Indeed, the presence of Paul's statement about political authority may be due to the fact that a close reading of the prophets and the life of Jesus could easily give the impression that political life is so corrupt that Christians are at liberty to disregard it or even overthrow it.

As a matter of fact it would be rare indeed for any Christian to obey the state whatever it demanded. Most Christians are highly selective with regard to what they consider to be the limit beyond which the state may not go. It is almost certain that, if the state forbade Christians to teach their children the truth about Jesus (and some states do try), the vast majority would disobey. There are other issues over which Christians, who otherwise would claim that the Church has no business to meddle in politics, are prepared to involve themselves. I am thinking of such matters as divorce, pornography, abortion and laws governing the use of Sunday.

Those Christians who accuse others of compromising the gospel, because they resist the aggression of the state against elementary human rights, such as freedom of assembly, liberty of the press, a fair and open trial on specific charges and access to the basic necessities of life, are indulging in sheer hypocrisy. It is one of the major tragedies of the Church's failure to witness consistently to Jesus that it is prepared to join issue with the state if it perceives its own rights and freedoms are under attack, but does nothing when those of other people are being threatened.

Finally, it should be noted that even in the Romans 13 passage Paul does not allow the state God's sanction for whatever it chooses to do. The probable interpretation of verse 6 is: 'The authorities are ministers of God *in so far as* they do these things.' They can cease to be God's servants and become his enemies by refusing to acknowledge any authority higher than their own and by abusing their power.

Christians are not permitted to resist the state as such, nor to set up their own parallel community outside the state, nor to attempt to control political power in their own interests. Their approach will concentrate on specific issues in which the central tenets of the gospel itself are being attacked. Only in those specific circumstances will they withdraw their support for the state.

Birth pangs of the new world

We return to the conviction that genuine suffering for the name is one of the principal evidences that the new age has dawned because of the coming of Jesus. The Christian community that suffers unjustly is a confirmation that the message about Jesus and the kingdom is good news. Jesus stated quite explicitly that the suffering of Christians is one of the principal signs that the kingdom of God is coming. The connection between the two is as close as that between leaves appearing on trees and the arrival of summer (Luke 21.29–31).

Human resistance to the reality of the new world is also part of the birth pangs of that world. That is why Christians, in spite of intense persecution, are encouraged to 'hold their heads high'. 'Liberation is near' (Luke 21.28).

In the course of 2000 years of history the major hallmark of the Christian, that which distinguishes faith from any other religious conviction, is the ability to suffer unjustly with joy and gladness and to face death triumphantly with a song of praise on the lips. Here is the supreme test of authentic commitment to the God and Father of Jesus Christ. Here is the most compelling evidence of the truth of the gospel.

'Who is sufficient for these things?' (2 Cor. 2.16; RSV).

Epilogue: Homage to the Ruler

This book has been about the task of the Christian community in the world today. It has tried to encourage a fresh look at the supreme responsibility of Christian people to spread the good news of God's kingdom in ways appropriate to the message itself. There is, however, a danger in placing too heavy an emphasis on what Christians should be doing – the danger of activism without serious reflection and without adequate time spent consciously with God.

Many Christian groups are activity-centred. This is quite natural, and in one way it is quite proper. Part of the process of radical change that people experience when they come to acknowledge Jesus as the centre of their lives is to have a renewed conscience. An awakened conscience can have a profound effect upon a person. When it is fed with the knowledge that it is a Christian's responsibility to live in a certain way, witness to neighbours and friends about Jesus Christ, become involved in programmes of care in the community, attend meetings to strengthen commitment, conscience impels us out into an endless round of worthy activities. We are aware there is so much (always more) to be done. Finding ourselves doing nothing very much may produce intense feelings of guilt, which, in turn, stop us being able to relax.

There is nothing wrong with an active conscience. Christians are in debt to others to help them discover the new world that Jesus has brought into being (Rom. 1.14–15): 'how terrible . . . if I did not preach the gospel!' (1 Cor. 9.16). And yet, activity alone, however noble and sacrificial, can easily degenerate into an end in itself. The Christian, rightly, is under pressure to perform: to show in practice that the message he believes is not just a neat arrangement of words. The pressure may build up in such a way that the disciple loses sight of the true end of every activity in the name of Jesus.

Instead of making all the tasks we are engaged in conscious acts of homage to the Creator and Redeemer of the universe, other lesser objectives are allowed to slip in. These may be the achievement of a balanced church programme, the number of books or magazines we read, the amount of money we give to agencies engaged in helping underprivileged or handicapped people, the people we visit or entertain, the pressure groups we work with. Each task is admirable. There is no sense of competition. We do not advocate a choice. We are simply arguing for a perspective and a context from which the tasks will flow in the right sequence and proportion.

Worship is, perhaps, the most basic human need and drive, though often not recognised and acknowledged. It is a universal phenomenon, existing in every culture. It responds to how human beings are. They are incapable, by nature, of ever being satisfied with what is perishable and transient. Hence, the great danger of substitution: of concentrating energies on the gifts of creation and the tasks given, rather than on the giver himself.

Everyone is bound to look for objects of some sort to admire, respect, enjoy and dedicate themselves to. People do not outgrow the desire to worship by becoming adult, or by changing their circumstances or way of thinking. They will from time to time probably shift their particular centre of concern. There is always some object present, however, that will focus their attention and motivate them either to follow, achieve or enjoy it.

Not all worship, unfortunately, is healthy and true (John 4.23). False worship is recognised in the Bible, called idolatry and strongly rebuked. It takes many forms and effects all kinds of people. A false outlook on life, however plausible and common it may be, is false worship: 'your heart will always be where your riches are' (Matt. 6.21). Idolatry is substitute worship: 'no one can be a slave of two masters . . . he will be loyal to one and despise the other' (Matt. 6.24).

It is an obvious fact of life that false-worship does not satisfy. We easily get tired both of our heroes and the objects of our desire. We either change them at regular intervals – trying everything to alleviate a deeper inner craving – or give them up in disillusionment. Some objects, however, can be very persistent, in particular possessions, prestige and power. Worship of God, on the other hand, grows always deeper and more fulfilling. The writer of the Psalm expresses the experience exactly: 'those who rush to other gods bring many troubles on themselves. . . . You, Lord, are all I have, and you give me all I need' (Ps. 16.4–5); 'what else have I in heaven but you? Since I have you, what else could I want on earth? . . . God is my strength; he is all I ever need' (Ps. 73.25–6).

In terms of the main subject of this book, there can be no kingdom without a king, no good news without Jesus, the Saviour, no concern for the poor without one who protects them in a special way. Evangelism has as its chief purpose the multiplication of worship, praise and thanksgiving to the King of kings and the Lord of lords. It is the vehicle for bringing people into a wholly new relationship with the One who reigns over the universe for ever.

Two attitudes in worship are equally applicable. The first is prostration. This gives a sense of being both a creature and unworthy. It is a physical position that acknowledges appropriately the majesty, glory and holy righteousness of God. It states a belief that God is high and exalted, dwelling in a place of burning, inextinguishable light; that there is no darkness nor inconsistency in what he does and wills; that he is the author of life in all its fullness and destroys all that brings death and chaos.

The second attitude is to hold the head high. It means we can look at God and speak to him face to face as a person speaks to their friend. Worship is to acknowledge that God is the one who forgives all our rebellions and cleanses us from all our faults, that he is our Father who runs towards us, embraces us as lost children when we return home from the wilderness and casts out all fear from our lives.

Worship is confessing who God is and letting him be God (Deut. 6.4–9; 11.13–21; Num. 15.37–41). It is praise to the one from whom all truth, goodness, beauty and harmony flow. It is rejoicing in the work of God's hands (Ps. 90.14–16). It is joy and confidence in the living God who has conquered death, deceit and doubt and opened up a new world to live in. Above all, worship is loving God with all we are and all we have, making everything available for him.

Though it is formalised from time to time in what we call acts of public worship, clearly worship is not confined to what is done in a church service, nor even in personal and corporate prayer. The pattern of community worship will include singing, prayer, prophecy, testimony, the reading, interpretation and application of God's Word and sharing together in a family meal. None of this, however, will have any meaning as a special act of worship apart from a pattern of life which is itself a continual offering to God (Col. 3.16–17).

Unless evangelism, seen as spreading everywhere the joyful good news of the kingdom for the poor, is itself an act of worship, of praise and thanksgiving, it is emptied of its true significance. Our whole reflection, therefore, on the need for all people to respond to the gospel and on the unavoidable challenge this places before all Christians must end on a note of homage to the one who alone is worthy to receive glory, honour and praise. The words of H. Bonar

sum up beautifully the concerns we have been trying so inadequately
to express:

> Fill Thou my life, O Lord my God,
> In every part with praise,
> That my whole being may proclaim
> Thy being and Thy ways.

> Fill every part of me with praise:
> Let all my being speak
> Of Thee and of Thy love, O Lord,
> Poor though I be and weak.

> So shalt Thou, God, from me, e'en me,
> Receive the glory due;
> And so shall I begin on earth
> The song for ever new.

Questions for discussion

Introduction

1. Why is the future so important for Christian faith?
2. What are the reasons for Christians believing only a part of the gospel? Do we fall into the same trap?

Chapter 1: The glories and follies of a passing age

1. Why are economic matters so crucial to the kind of life we lead?
2. From a Christian perspective what have been the main achievements and threats of modern science?
3. In what ways is our economic system incompatible with a biblically based view of the world?
4. Why does Marxism promise more than it is able to accomplish?

Chapter 2: Signs of panic and signs of hope

1. In what ways does aggression among nations show itself?
2. What are the real issues at stake in the argument about abortion?
3. Why should Christians be divided over the question of nuclear deterrence?

Chapter 3: Why the tide has turned

1. Why has the theme of God's kingdom come to the fore in many Christian circles today?
2. How correct do you think Marxists are in their criticism of modern societies?
3. How should Christians respond to the challenge of Marxism?

Chapter 4: Exploring the interior

1. What are the essential elements of God's kingdom as recorded in the Old Testament?
2. What did Jews of Jesus' time believe about the kingdom?

3. Why did Jesus' teaching about the kingdom not fit in with current views?
4. How would you explain the meaning of the kingdom to an interested non-Christian?

Chapter 5: Luxury apartments and desolate slums

1. How should a Christian react to inequality among people?
2. How does one explain the continuance of poverty in a world with so many resources?
3. What kind of changes are needed to reduce poverty?

Chapter 6: Who cares about Copacabana?

1. What do you understand to be the biblical attitude to wealth?
2. In what ways do we fail to follow biblical teaching on wealth in practice?
3. In what ways should Christians be prepared to share the wealth they have?

Chapter 7: That the hungry may be filled with good things

1. How do you react to what *other* people call extreme views?
2. What kinds of action can Christians take to aid development?
3. What do you think are the merits and the problems of a social wage?

Chapter 8: A battle for the traditions of the elders?

1. How would you react on being told you did not fully understand the gospel?
2. How would you explain the gospel in terms of God's kingdom?
3. Why is universalism incompatible with the message of Christ?

Chapter 9: Good news for outsiders

1. Why is it difficult to define evangelism satisfactorily?
2. Why should the poor be more attracted to the gospel?
3. If the poor are the main recipients of the gospel, how should this affect our evangelistic strategy?
4. Why is social action done in Christ's name part of evangelism?

Chapter 10: How should the messengers go?

1. Does it really matter what means we use as long as people respond to the gospel?
2. How can you gain more confidence in presenting the case for Christian faith?
3. In what way is the Church part of the gospel?
4. How can your church break new ground in evangelism?

Chapter 11: A family with a difference

1. What does it mean for your church to be a servant-community in its neighbourhood?
2. How can the unique Christian sense of belonging to one another be fostered in your fellowship?
3. Do you think the suggestions about leadership should be implemented?

Chapter 12: Through suffering to the kingdom

1. Why is Jesus' death the key to all suffering?
2. In what ways would you expect Christians to suffer because of their faith?
3. Is there something wrong with the Church, if it is not being persecuted?
4. Why is suffering for Christ's sake evidence that God's kingdom is present?

Epilogue: Homage to the Ruler

1. Why should all our activities be made into acts of worship to God?
2. In what ways are you tempted to engage in false-worship?
3. How can worship and evangelism be more closely united?

Appendix: A statement of concerns on the future of the Lausanne Committee for World Evangelisation

During the 1974 Lausanne Congress on World Evangelisation it was affirmed that 'Evangelism and socio-political involvement are both part of our Christian duty'. The Congress also asserted that 'we should share God's concern for justice and reconciliation throughout human society and for the liberation of men from every kind of oppression' (*Lausanne Covenant*, section 5).

During the six years since the Lausanne Congress convened, the 'Lausanne Spirit' has stimulated world evangelisation and has devised useful tools for evangelisation. The Strategy Working Group has ably promoted the awareness of the need to reach people–groups and has devised useful strategies for doing so. The Theology and Education Group must be commended for sponsoring the International Consultation (Willowbank, Bermuda, 1978) which produced the *Willowbank Report on Gospel and Culture* and for co-sponsoring with the Theological Commission of the World Evangelical Fellowship the International Consultation on Simple Life Style (High Leigh, England, March 1980) which produced *An Evangelical Commitment to Simple Lifestyle,* which contains a call to work for justice.

It is a fact, nevertheless, that outside of these noble and commendable efforts the Lausanne Committee for World Evangelisation (LCWE) does not seem to have been seriously concerned with the social, political and economic issues in many parts of the world that are a great stumbling block to the proclamation of the gospel. This is clearly evident here at Pattaya, Thailand, during this Consultation on World Evangelisation. We have a working group on 'Reaching Refugees', but none on those that are largely responsible for the refugee situation around the world: politicians, armed forces, freedom fighters, national oligarchies and the controllers of international economic power.

Since the world is made up not just of people–groups but of institutions and structures, the Lausanne Movement, if it is to make a lasting and profound evangelistic impact in the six continents of the world, must make a special effort to help Christians, local churches, denominations and mission agencies to identify not only people–groups but also the social, economic and political institutions that determine their lives and the structures behind them that hinder evangelism. Indeed to be an effective mobilising agent for the evangelisation of the world the LCWE (as the visible expression of the Lausanne Movement) will have to give guidelines to Christians in many parts of the world who are wrestling with the problems of racial, tribal and sexual discrimination, political imperialism, economic exploitation, and physical and psychological harassment of totalitarian regimes (of whatever ideology) (i.e. tortures, unjust imprisonment and forced exiles) and the liberation struggles that are the consequences of such violent aggression.

With sadness and tears we must note that there are Christians in and outside of South Africa who claim to be Bible-believing Christians and give implicit or explicit support to apartheid. We recognise, however, that there are other evangelicals who have taken a courageous stance against this evil. There are evangelicals in Latin America and Asia that claim to be true followers of Jesus Christ and yet give direct or indirect support to the growing number of repressive anti-democratic governments on these continents. Similarly there are evangelical leaders in some communist-ruled countries who appear to support uncritically their governments even when they deny basic human rights (including freedom of religion). And everywhere else in the world, but particularly in North America, Western Europe and Australasia there are many evangelical Christians who support (some directly, many unwittingly) the economic dominations of the poor nations of the world by the economic policies of the developed nations and the activities of multi-national corporations. Those evangelicals that lend their support to these practices are a great scandal to the evangelical witness in general and to the evangelisation of the poor people of the earth in particular. The LCWE should give guidance on how these evangelicals can be reached with the whole biblical gospel and be challenged to repent and work for justice.

Evangelicals should not blindly condemn liberation movements. Rather they should seek to give sound biblical bases for the creation of just alternative societies.

The LCWE should exhort heads of nations and other government officials who claim to be Christians to set an example by being 'just and righteous' in the exercise of their office. This would remove a major stumbling block to evangelism in many countries.

The LCWE should exhort evangelicals around the world to proclaim the gospel in word and deed, 'in season and out of season' to all the unreached people. But it should do so bearing in mind that the overwhelming majority of them are the poor and the powerless and the oppressed of the earth. The God of the gospel not only speaks (Heb. 1.1) but sees the condition of the oppressed (Exod. 2.35) and hears their cry (Exod. 3.7; Acts 7.34; Jas. 5.1–5). Jesus himself set the example of an authentic evangelisation by proclaiming the gospel to the poor in word and deeds (Matt. 11.4—6).

For these reasons, we urge that the LCWE be given a mandate to continue with its ministry and implement the following recommendations:

1. That the LCWE reaffirm its commitment to all aspects of the Lausanne Covenant, and in particular provide new leadership to help evangelicals to implement its call to social responsibility as well as evangelism.
2. That the LCWE encourage and promote the formation of study groups at all levels, to deal with social, political and economic issues, and provide specific guidance on how evangelicals can effectively apply the Lausanne Covenant's affirmation of 'God's concern for justice and reconciliation throughout human society and liberation of men from every kind of oppression'.
3. That within the next three years the LCWE convene a World Congress on Social Responsibility and its implications for evangelisation.
4. That the LCWE give guidelines on how evangelicals who support oppression and discrimination (thus hindering evangelism) can be reached by the gospel and challenged to repent and uphold biblical truth, and how to give encouragement and support to Christians of all races in situations of oppression as they are seeking to be faithful to the gospel at a great risk.

We, the undersigned, present this statement to the LCWE Executive Committee to take appropriate action.

[Then followed something over 200 signatures, which were collected in a little over 24 hours, about one-third of the participants at COWE. A covering letter to Dr Leighton Ford, the Chairman of the LCWE Executive Committee, was signed by the following seven people, who were also responsible for the final draft of the statement: Orlando Costas, Bishop David Gitari, C. L. Hilliard, J. A. Kirk, Peter Kuzmic, Vinay Samuel and Ron Sider.]

Biblical references

Index

Select bibliography

The purpose of the following list of books and articles is to serve as a resource-guide for any who may be interested in following up further any of the discussion developed in the course of this book.

The choice of titles does not in any way exhaust the many books that deal with the points I have raised. I have, however, tried to be fair to various viewpoints where controversial issues have been touched upon. This means that I do not cite a book because I am necessarily in agreement with the author's main position; rather, because it represents a viewpoint held by people who have argued a case with integrity.

The listing of books by chapter is intended to suggest some of the important works available that touch on the same subject-matter. A number of books clearly cover issues that I deal with over several chapters and, therefore, would readily fit elsewhere as well.

Introduction

Armerding and Gasque, *Dreams, Visions and Oracles* (Baker, Grand Rapids, 1977).

Bosch, *Witness to the World: The Christian Mission in Theological Perspective* (Marshall Morgan & Scott, Basingstoke, 1980).

'The Chicago Statement on Biblical Inerrancy', *Themelios*, vol. 4, no. 3 (April 1979), pp. 104–6.

Costas, *The Integrity of Mission* (Harper & Row, New York, 1979).

Costas, *Christ Outside the Gate: Mission beyond Christendom* (Orbis Books, New York, 1982).

de Santa Ana, *Towards a Church of the Poor* (WCC Geneva, 1979).

Douglas (ed.), *Let the Earth Hear His Voice* (World Wide Publications, Minneapolis, 1975).

Hoekstra, *Evangelism in Eclipse: World Mission and the World Council of Churches* (Paternoster Press, Exeter, 1979).

Johnston, *The Battle for World Evangelism* (Tyndale House, Wheaton, 1978).

Lindsell, *The Battle for the Bible* (Zondervan, Grand Rapids, 1977).

Lindsell, *The Bible in the Balance* (Zondervan, Grand Rapids, 1979).

Lindsey, *The Late Great Planet Earth* (Lakeland, London, 1971).

Lindsey, *There's a New World Coming* (Zondervan, Grand Rapids, 1973).

Stott, *The Lausanne Covenant: An Exposition and Commentary* (World Wide Publications, Minneapolis, 1975).

Travis, *I Believe in the Second Coming of Christ* (Hodder & Stoughton, London, 1982).

Chapter 1

D. Beckmann, *Where Faith and Economics Meet: A Christian Critique* (Augsburg Publishing House, Minneapolis, 1981).

Fusfield, *Economics* (Heath & Co., Toronto, 1972).

Goudzwaard, *Capitalism and Progress* (Eerdmans, Grand Rapids, 1980).

Griffiths, *Morality in the Market Place* (Hodder & Stoughton, London, 1982).

Hay, *A Christian Critique of Capitalism* (Grove Booklets, Nottingham, 1975).

Hay, *A Christian Critique of Socialism* (Grove Booklets, Nottingham, 1982).

Oden, *Agenda for Theology: Recovering Christian Roots* (Harper & Row, San Francisco, 1979).

Preston, *Religion and the Persistence of Capitalism* (SCM, London, 1979).

Sleeman, *Economic Crisis: A Christian Perspective* (SCM, London, 1976).

Chapter 2

Abrecht and Koshy, *Before It's Too Late: The Challenge of Nuclear Disarmament* (WCC, Geneva, 1983).

Barker, Kreider, Nobbs, Scott and Sweatman, *Time to Choose: A Grass Roots Study Guide on the Nuclear Arms Race from a Christian Perspective.* (Lytchett Minister, 1983 Celebration).

Cook, *The Moral Maze: A Way of Exploring Christian Ethics* (SPCK, London, 1983).

Harries (ed.), *What Hope in an Armed World?* (Pickering & Inglis, Basingstoke, 1982).

McCormick, *How Brave a New World? Dilemmas in Bioethics* (SCM, London, 1981).

Mzrui, *The African Condition* (BBC Publications, London, 1980).

Schaeffer and Koop, *Whatever Happened to the Human Race?* (Revell, New Jersey, 1979).

Shaftesbury Project, *Handbook on World Development* (Nottingham, 1983).

Sider and Taylor, *Nuclear Holocaust and Christian Hope* (IVP, Downers Grove, and Paulist Press, New York, 1983).

Stott (ed.), *The Year 2000* (Marshall Morgan & Scott, Basingstoke, 1983).

Chapter 3

Camara, *The Conversions of a Bishop* (Collins, London, 1979).

Camara, *Thomas Aquinas and Karl Marx* (CIIR, London, 1982).

de Gruchy, *The Church Struggle in South Africa* (Eerdmans, Grand Rapids, 1979).

Kendall, *The End of an Era: Africa and the Missionary* (SPCK, London, 1978).

Lash, *A Matter of Hope: A Theologian's Reflections on the Thought of K. Marx* (Darton, Longman & Todd, London, 1981).

Leech, *The Social God* (Sheldon Press, London, 1981).

Lyon, *Karl Marx: A Christian Biography* (IVP, Leicester, 1981).

Marstin, *Beyond Our Tribal Gods: The Maturing of Faith* (Orbis Books, New York, 1979).

McLellan, *Marxism after Marx* (Macmillan, London, 1979).

Miranda, *Marx against the Marxists: The Christian Humanism of Karl Marx* (SCM, London, 1980).

Samuel and Sugden (eds.), *Sharing Jesus in the Two-Thirds World* (PIM, Bangalore, 1983).

WCC, *Your Kingdom Come* (WCC, Geneva, 1982).

Wilczynski, *Marxism, Socialism and Communism* (Macmillan, London, 1981).

Worsley, *Marx and Marxism* (Horwood & Tavistock, London, 1982).

Chapter 4

Baird, *The Justice of God in the Teaching of Jesus* (SCM, London, 1963).
Flusser, *Jesus* (Herder & Herder, New York, 1969).
Marshall, 'The Kingdom of God', in *Zondervan Pictorial Encyclopaedia of the Bible*, vol. III, pp. 801–9.
Perrin, *Jesus and the Language of the Kingdom*, (SCM, London, 1976).
Piper, *Love your Enemies* (CUP, London, 1979).
Riches, *Jesus and the Transformation of Judaism* (Darton, Longman & Todd, London, 1980).
Sobrino, *Christology at the Crossroads: A Latin American Approach* (SCM, London, 1980).

Chapter 5

Alison, article in *Christian Graduate*, vol. 32, no. 4 (1979).
de Santa Ana (ed.), *Separation without Hope: The Church and the Poor during the Industrial Revolution and Colonial Expansion* (Orbis Books, New York, 1978).
Elliott, *The Development Debate* (SCM, London, 1971).
Justice and Peace Commission, *Sao Paolo: Growth and Poverty* (Bowerdean Press, London, 1978).
Kurien, *Poverty, Planning and Social Transformation* (Allied Publishers, Bombay, 1978).
May, *The Third World Calamity* (Routledge & Kegan Paul, London, 1981).

Chapter 6

Boerma, *Rich Man, Poor Man, and the Bible* (SCM, London, 1979).
de Santa Ana, *Good News to the Poor: The Challenge of the Poor in the History of the Church* (WCC, Geneva, 1977).
de Vaux, *Ancient Israel: Its Life and Institutions* (Darton, Longman & Todd, London, 1974).
Hanks, *Oppression, Poverty and Liberation: Biblical Reflections* (Orbis Books, New York, 1983).
Hengel, *Property and Riches in the Early Church* (SCM, London, 1974).
Mealand, *Poverty and Expectation in the Gospels* (SPCK, London, 1980).
Miranda, *Communism in the Bible* (SCM, London, 1982).

Chapter 7

Balogh, *The Economics of Poverty* (Weidenfeld & Nicolson, London, 1974).
Batchelor, *People in Rural Development* (Paternoster Press, Exeter, 1981).

Bleakley, *In Place of Work . . . The Sufficient Society: A Study of Technology from the Point of View of People* (SCM, London, 1981).

McGinnis, *Bread and Justice: Toward a New International Economic Order* (Paulist Press, New York, 1979).

Oldham. *Christianity and the Race Problem* (SCM, London, 1926).

Riddell, *Restructuring British Industry: The Third World Dimension* (CIIR, London, 1979).

Seabrook, 'Mrs Thatcher has shown that what has happened within the Left over the last 30 years was all fiction', *The Guardian*, 1st March (1982), p. 7.

Sinclair, *Green Finger of God* (Paternoster Press, Exeter, 1980).

Sine (ed.), *The Church in Response to Human Need* (MARC, Monrovia, 1983).

Chapter 8

Cotterell, *The Eleventh Commandment: Church and Mission Today* (IVP, Leicester, 1981).

John Paul II, *Redemptor Hominis* (Catholic Truth Society, London, 1979).

Krass, *Five Lanterns at Sundown: Evangelism in a Chastened Mood* (Eerdmans, Grand Rapids, 1978).

Moberg, *The Great Reversal: Evangelism vs Social Concern* (Scripture Union, London, 1972).

Sine, *The Mustard Seed Conspiracy* (Word Books, Waco, 1981).

Stott (ed.), *Evangelism and Social Responsibility: An Evangelical Commitment (The Grand Rapids Report)* (Paternoster Press, Exeter, 1982).

Wallis, *The Call to Conversion* (Lion, Tring, 1981).

Chapter 9

McGavran, 'The Dimensions of World Evangelisation', in Douglas (ed.), *Let the Earth Hear His Voice* (cf. under Introduction).

McGavran (ed.), *The Eye of the Storm: The Great Debate in Mission* (Word Books, Waco, 1972).

Newbigin, *The Open Secret* (SPCK, London, 1978).

Newbigin, 'Cross-currents in Ecumenical and Evangelical Understandings of Mission', *IBMR*, vol. 6, no. 4 (October 1982), pp. 146-51.

Scott, *Bring Forth Justice: A Contemporary Perspective on Mission* (Eerdmans, Grand Rapids, 1980).

Wagner, 'Response', *IBMR*, vol. 6, no. 4 (October 1982), pp. 148-9.

Chapter 10

Miguez, *Christians and Marxists: The Mutual Challenge to Revolution* (Hodder & Stoughton, London, 1976).
Padilla, 'The Unity of the Church and the Homogeneous Unit Principle', *IBMR*, vol. 6 (January 1982), pp. 23-30.
Petersen, *Evangelism as Lifestyle* (Navpress, Colorado Springs, 1980).

Chapter 11

ARCIC, *The Final Report* (SPCK and CTS, London, 1982).
Clark, *Basic Communities: Towards an Alternative Society* (SPCK, London, 1977).
Harper, *Let My People Grow* (Hodder & Stoughton, London, 1977).
Jeremias, *New Testament Theology* (SCM, London, 1971).
Kirk, 'Did Officials in the New Testament Receive a Salary?', *ET*, vol. LXXXIV, no. 4 (January 1973).
Kirk, 'A New Way of Being the Church', *Grass-Roots*, vol. 9, no. 3 (May/June 1983).
Lima Report, *Baptism, Eucharist and Ministry* (WCC, Geneva, 1982).
Mellis, *Committed Communities: Fresh Streams for World Missions* (William Carey Library, Pasadena, 1976).
Moltmann, *The Open Church: Invitation to a Messianic Lifestyle* (SCM, London, 1978).
Torres and Eagleson, *The Challenge of Basic Christian Communities* (Orbis Books, New York, 1981).

Chapter 12

Blamires, *A God Who Acts: Recognizing the Hand of God in Suffering and Failure* (SPCK, London, 1983).
Dehqani-Tafti, *The Hard Awakening* (SPCK, London, 1981).
Dewar, *All for Christ* (OUP, London, 1980).
Ford, *Janani, The Making of a Martyr* (Marshall Morgan & Scott, Basingstoke, 1978).
Hebblethwaite, *Evil, Suffering and Religion* (Sheldon Press, London, 1976).
Hunt, *Inside Iran* (Lion, Tring, 1981).
Jerez, *The Church in Central America* (CIIR, London, 1981).
Romero and Sobrino, *Romero: Martyr for Liberation* (CIIR, London, 1982).
Wooding and Barnett, *Uganda Holocaust* (Pickering & Inglis, London, 1980).